Struggle and
Suffrage in Sheffield:
1850–1950

Struggle and Suffrage in Sheffield: 1850–1950

Margaret Drinkall

PEN & SWORD HISTORY

AN IMPRINT OF PEN & SWORD BOOKS LTD.
YORKSHIRE – PHILADELPHIA

First published in Great Britain in 2018 by
Pen & Sword History
An imprint of Pen & Sword Books Ltd
Yorkshire – Philadelphia

Copyright © Margaret Drinkall, 2018

ISBN 9781526712745

The right of Margaret Drinkall to be identified as Author of this work has been asserted by her in accordance with the Copyright, Designs and Patents Act 1988.

A CIP catalogue record for this book is available from the British Library.

Typeset in 11.5/13.5 point Times NR MT by SRJ Info Jnana System Pvt Ltd.

Printed and bound in England by CPI Group (UK) Ltd, Croydon, CR0 4YY

Pen & Sword Books Limited incorporates the imprints of Atlas, Archaeology, Aviation, Discovery, Family History, Fiction, History, Maritime, Military, Military Classics, Politics, Select, Transport, True Crime, Air World, Frontline Publishing, Leo Cooper, Remember When, Seaforth Publishing, The Praetorian Press, Wharncliffe Local History, Wharncliffe Transport, Wharncliffe True Crime and White Owl.

For a complete list of Pen & Sword titles please contact
PEN & SWORD BOOKS LIMITED
47 Church Street, Barnsley, South Yorkshire, S70 2AS, England
E-mail: enquiries@pen-and-sword.co.uk
Website: www.pen-and-sword.co.uk

Or

PEN & SWORD BOOKS LIMITED
1950 Lawrence Rd, Havertown, PA 19083, USA
E-mail: Uspen-and-sword@casematepublishers.com
Website: www.penandswordbooks.com

Introduction and Acknowledgements

From 1850 onwards Sheffield had become a town of great expansion thanks to the steel, cutlery and associated trades, and consequently had gained a reputation as being a very radical city. Great religious and reform movements had been started or took root in Sheffield, such as the working-class movement for political reform that became known as Chartism, led by Samuel Holberry. What was less known was that other equally radical movements such as the movement against slavery, as well as the earliest demand for equal rights in 1851, were led by women. History shows that Sheffield women rose to the occasion when required, whether it was in the formation of women's patrols, or as court missionaries, they took the lead. But it was the Sheffield suffragettes who put the city on the map. Unable to gain the vote by peaceful means, these ordinary women became militant to gain their ends. By using such tactics as storming meetings, wrestling with police constables or blowing up pillar boxes, the women of the city showed their determination to gain the vote.

Yet prior to 1850 women were generally powerless and subservient to male authority. Seen as the property of her husband, one Sheffield wife found herself sold in the market place without her consent. Women could not speak in public and had no say in civic matters, as all positions of power and authority were dominated by men. As a sex they were invisible and in most cases the only time they were mentioned in local newspapers was when they were brought into court. Yet throughout two world wars Sheffield women proved again and again that they were the equal of men. It was not until the new century dawned that they would eventually break the mould and become truly emancipated. Slowly but surely they were elected onto various boards and committees, made speeches and became better educated before finally breaking into the ranks of male dominance, the City Council itself.

Many people have been involved in the writing of this book. Firstly I would like to thank Jeannette Hensby, a fellow author, for her continued advice and support which is very much appreciated. I would have found this book very difficult to research without help from Alice Collins, who allowed me to have free access to her own extensive research materials. I would also like to offer my gratitude to Nancy Fielder, editor of the *Star* and *Sheffield Telegraph* for permission to reproduce many of the illustrations in the book. My grateful thanks also go to Gladys Brand (nee Wakefield) one of the original 'Women of Steel' for her invaluable contribution, and for permission to publish her photographs. I would also like to thank Ralph Darlington of Salford University for permission to use excerpts from the Mollie Murphy book. As always I was most grateful for the help given to me by the staff at the Sheffield Archive and Local Studies Department. My thanks also to Amy Jordan and the production team at Pen & Sword, and to Janet Wood for her editing. Finally, as always, thanks to my son Chris for all his IT skills, help and encouragement.

Contents

CHAPTER ONE

Love and Marriage

Anyone reading a newspaper in the years from 1850 to 1900 could be forgiven for thinking that in Sheffield, as in other towns and cities throughout Britain, most women were invisible. All the most responsible city positions, the town council, the legal authorities, the guardians of the workhouse or any position of power and authority were all run by men. Women had no say in either the law of the land or the development of the towns and cities in which they lived. Occasionally the names of prominent females were mentioned in the Sheffield newspapers such as the Lady Mayoress, Mistress Cutler or the aristocratic Lady Fitzwilliam, but they were only mentioned when handing out prizes or attending philanthropic events. In the Victorian patriarchal society most women knew their place, and the subjection of the women to men was given validity by the Bible itself. In society's eyes, as a female child you were under the jurisdiction of your father which continued until you were married, and then it was automatically transferred to your husband. Some women might have thought that freedom could only be obtained through marriage, however, the reality was that marriage held little freedom for women who could be sold like cattle if their husbands so desired. One woman had found out exactly how powerless she was when, on the morning of 12 January 1847, she found herself being sold in the Sheffield market place. Although this act was basically criminal, it underlined the law that a woman was the property of the man, and therefore could be sold by him like a piece of meat.

The disgusting affair came to light when the Mayor of Sheffield, Edward Vickers was on his way to the Town Hall, when he noticed that the market day crowd was much more extensive than usual. He made enquiries into the matter and when he was told that the crowds were there to see a 'wife sale', he ordered police officers to bring the pair before him. However, by the time they returned the man had absconded and only the woman was brought into the court room. She showed signs of great distress, sobbing bitterly as she told the bench that her name was Harriet Trotter and she was the wife of Robert Trotter. She explained that although they had been married for only twelve months, during that time her husband had treated her so cruelly that she had been forced to take him before the magistrates. Because of this, her husband informed her that he intended selling her to one of his workmates. Mrs Trotter said that Robert had a gun and had threatened to shoot her if she did not go through with the sale, and so great was her alarm that she had been forced to agree. She did not know the man into whose possession she was to be passed. The mayor asked that a warrant be issued for the husband. The next morning Robert Trotter appeared completely unrepentant when he was brought before the magistrates, who castigated him for his behaviour. However disgusted he felt at the circumstances, the mayor had little option but to order him to find sureties to keep the peace for the next six months and the couple left the court together.

Although we have a very different view today, in the Victorian period domestic violence within a marriage was socially acceptable. The religious ideal that a woman must follow the lead of her husband, appeared to give him a God-given right to punish his wife for her imagined transgressions. By law a man had a right to chastise his wife providing he used an implement no bigger than his thumb, which is where the saying 'rule of thumb' came from. As a result of this, numerous husbands were brought before the Sheffield magistrates' court charged with assault on their wives. One particular violent case of domestic abuse left the court gasping as a wife spoke about her treatment at her husband's hands. On 20 July 1871 a

Magistrates' Court Sheffield where cases of domestic abuse were regularly heard.

powerful-looking man named Charles Dent was brought into court, charged with assaulting his wife, Mary Jane Dent. The woman looked pale and emaciated when giving evidence that on the previous Monday she had gone to a neighbours begging for a cup of tea, as she had had nothing to eat for two days. The neighbour made her a drink, but before she could taste it her husband returned home drunk. He ordered her to go home and as soon as he got her into the house he struck her on the side of the head with a poker. Neighbours crowded around the house to try and help her, but the prisoner threatened as to what he would do to them if they did not go away. The police were called and the woman was only then rescued and taken to the workhouse, with her husband's threats ringing in her ears. Mrs Dent had been examined by one of the medical officers of the workhouse, Dr Kemp, on the previous afternoon, and he told the bench that he found her suffering from the effects of ill usage and want of proper food, indeed food of any kind. He said that because of this she was in a very exhausted and debilitated state. The woman had told him that on the day of the offence, Dent had taken the last 3s in the house and had used it to get drunk. Mrs Dent said that in the past he had tried to get her to prostitute herself or steal for him, but she refused to do it. Neighbours confirmed the woman's story and said that the couple were living in furnished property, although every piece of furniture in the house had been smashed. In his defence the prisoner tried to maintain that his wife had attacked him on occasions, but the mayor told him that:

> a poor weak, half-starved woman such as your wife would be hardly likely to attack a brute like you. If you had a dog you would have treated it better than you had done your poor delicate wife. But for the interference of the neighbours you might have murdered her.

Warning Dent that he was lucky he was not before the bench on a much more serious charge, the prisoner was sentenced to six months imprisonment with hard labour at Wakefield Gaol. It was recorded that 'the decision was received with much satisfaction by the spectators in court'. What happened to such women when the prison sentence had been served and she was once more at her husband's mercy was left unrecorded. However, domestic abuse was becoming so prevalent that the government was forced to step in and look at ways in which women should be protected, even from their own husbands.

Divorce was expensive and so it was out of the question for ordinary women until the Matrimonial Causes Act of 1878 was introduced, when some Sheffield women were at last able to gain some slight protection from their abusive husbands. One such local case was brought before the Divorce Division of the High Court of Justice, one of the most senior courts in England, in March 1880. It was that of a Mrs Martha Jackson who brought a petition asking for a judicial separation from her husband, Mr Thomas Jackson who had been the proprietor of the Pavilion Music Hall in Sheffield. The court was told that the couple had married on 5 September 1854 and had lived together until May 1878. He was reported to be of 'very intemperate habits' and constantly assaulted his wife. Mrs Jackson claimed that he had threatened her so violently that she had been forced to flee the marital home and stay with relatives. She stated that her husband had threatened to break her neck 'were it not for the law' and had repeatedly struck her in the face and told her to leave the house. Mr Jackson did not appear at the court, but filed a report claiming that he had lived under extreme provocation from his wife. Witnesses gave statements about several incidents of cruelty, before Sir R.J. Phillimore granted Mrs Jackson a decree of judicial separation.

The same Act meant that working-class women were now able to get a judicial separation from local magistrates such as that of a Sheffield sculptor in September 1881. Theophilus Smith of Thirlwell Road, Heeley was arrested for committing an aggravated assault on his wife Mrs Louisa Smith and his 14-year-old daughter, Ethel. Her solicitor told the court that there was a history of assaults and that Smith had been brought before the bench on several occasions, the last being in May of that year. He had been bound over to keep the peace, which had expired on 25 August when he assaulted his wife again causing her to leave the house overnight. When she returned the next day Smith was lying on the couch in a state of inebriation. Inevitably it was not long before the couple argued once more and he tried to put her out of the house. The little girl Ellen tried to help her mother, but her father twisted her fingers so severely that she too was forced to leave the house. Mrs Smith gave evidence that she was afraid that her husband would kill her when he was drunk, and as a consequence she was staying at her father's house. Young Ethel Smith and other witnesses were brought to support Mrs Smith's statement. Mr Smith's solicitor claimed that the assaults were not aggravated, but that he too had claimed provocation to be the reasons for the beatings. The solicitor assured the magistrates that if they refused her application and she returned back to live with her husband again, her life would not be in danger. The court adjourned for quarter of an hour before the magistrates agreed that

Mrs Smith's life would indeed be in danger if she returned to live with her husband. They fined him £5 and costs for the assaults, and ordered him to pay £1 a week to maintain herself and her four children. Mr Smith was also ordered to keep the peace for three months under sureties of £20. Her solicitor then made an astonishing claim that whilst Mr Smith had been at his office, he had made threats against himself if he continued with his wife's claim and added that 'he was himself most afraid of him'. The bench re-considered and increased Mr Smith's sureties to £50 to keep the peace. Although Mrs Smith might have gained some respite from her cruel husband, she would no doubt have found it very difficult to keep herself and four children under ten years of age on £1 a week. Married women with dependent children had little options for employment, apart from undertaking other women's domestic chores for a pittance.

As we have seen, even married women had few legal rights, being regarded as the property of their husband, therefore anything she owned automatically belonged to him. He had the right to take any property which his wife had or any earnings that she made. However, after the Married Women's Property Act of 1870 a man could not take his wife's earnings, but it was not until the Act of 1882 that married women were given the same rights as unmarried women, to own, buy and sell their own property. More importantly to women was the fact that, at last, their legal identity was seen as being separate to that of their husband. Nevertheless there were still cases of husbands using violence to gain their wives' inheritance.

A case of a Sheffield woman whose husband had threatened to kick her to death if she did not hand over to him her legacy of £21, was heard before Sheffield magistrates on 14 March 1911. Mrs Emma Blagdon of Sutton Street, Sheffield applied for a separation order on the grounds of her husband's persistent cruelty. She told the bench that she had been married for twelve years and there were seven children from the marriage, the youngest being only eight months old. Mrs Blagdon stated that although she had been granted a separation order in November last, the allowance which the magistrates had ordered had not been enough, and she had been forced to return to him. She claimed that since then the situation for her had become worse and worse. Her husband had spent £64 in the previous five weeks on horse racing and every time he lost he was most violent to her. If she remonstrated with him, he struck and kicked her and had also struck at the baby who had been sitting on her knee. The £21 had been left to Mrs Blagdon by her recently-deceased husband's sister who, when told that she was dying, came to live with the family, and the sum was some small recompense for the nursing she had received from her sister-in-law. Mrs Blagdon had given her husband a sovereign, but later the same day he had demanded the rest from her and she was so afraid of him that she left the house. She told the magistrates that she wanted to use the money to train as a midwife, so that she could earn enough money to keep herself and her children. Mr Blagdon was called into court and he told the bench that the sum of money had been a bone of contention between the couple. He denied kicking or threatening her, but admitted that he had struck her once or twice and declared 'she is always nagging'. However, the magistrates saw the wife's point of view, and an order was made for the husband to pay 12s a week to his wife and she was to retain the custody of the children.

Throughout the years 1850–1950 many Sheffield working-class couples interpreted the law on marriage and divorce quite flexibly. As we have seen, for financial reasons a woman had little option but to find a man to provide for her, and a father who had lost his wife needed someone to look after his children. This interdependency often resulted in couples tending to 'live in sin' rather than divorce. The courts and indeed the community at large took a more lenient view on this subject, but when the couple took it further and the crime of bigamy occurred, then the matter was forced upon the legal authorities and they had to take action.

Such an instance happened in March 1850 when a man called Henry Bayley was brought before the judge, Mr Baron Rolfe, at the assizes in Leeds. He had been charged with marrying another woman whilst his former wife was still alive. The jury was told

The chair from where Mr Baron Rolfe heard the bigamy case against Henry Bayley in March 1850.

that he had married his first wife Eliza Bedford in 1843 and they had lived together for two years. Then in 1849 he contracted a second illegal marriage at Sheffield to a woman called Eliza Maxfield. When the second Eliza was informed that he was a married man she refused to believe it, until it was confirmed by her 'husband's' brother. Bayley was quickly found guilty and transported for seven years. A well-used defence in such cases was that the errant party had not seen their previous partner for seven years and therefore assumed they were dead.

As the century rolled on, some sympathy was demonstrated by the legal authorities and more lenient sentences were passed for the crime of bigamy. An illustration of this was when a 32-year-old Sheffield woman was charged with two counts of bigamy at Leeds Assizes on 25 May 1892 when she only received four months imprisonment. Sarah Ann Newboult told the judge that she had married her first husband at Everton near Bawtry in 1881 before marrying again in August 1888 to Henry Blaymires at Sheffield. Newboult obviously enjoyed getting married, as she then went through a third ceremony with a man named Briggs in April 1892 after telling him that she was a widow, her two previous husbands being accidentally killed. Newboult said that her first husband had treated her so badly that she had attempted to poison herself, and had been sent to a criminal lunatic asylum for six months. There she found herself a job as a nurse and supported herself until she met Blaymires with whom she lived for four years before agreeing to marry him. After they were married he too ill-treated her, before leaving her with nothing to eat and she was forced to sell all her furniture to buy food. She told the judge that Briggs, unlike the other two husbands, had always treated her well. Nevertheless the judge castigated her for deceiving this good man before sentencing her to one year's imprisonment with hard labour.

It was estimated that the displacement of records during the Great War made it easier to commit bigamy. Such a case was heard at Sheffield Police Court on 31 March 1916. James Hillman, a soldier in one of the camps, was arrested and charged with bigamously marrying Ethel Bradley of Fawley Road, Sheffield. She was a widow whose husband had been killed at Neuve Chappelle in March 1915. The woman told the court that the prisoner had told her that he was a single man and that he had been fighting in France for the previous twelve months. They were married on 12 February at the Ecclesall Registry Office. She had no idea that he was married until she went to the barracks for a separation allowance, and it was the army authorities who informed her that he was a married man. His wife also appeared at the court with a baby in her arms and told the bench that the couple had been married at Shelton near Stoke-on-Trent in 1912 and had two children. They had lived together until April 1915 when he enlisted, although he had several times deserted from his regiment. The first Mrs Hillman was complaining that her husband had sold the house over her head, when the prisoner interrupted, and stated that he had only done it because she went with other men. His wife denied this and told the court that she had several times given him money to return back to his regiment, which he had instead spent on drink. The prisoner was sent to take his trial at the assizes, where in May 1916 he received a sentence of twelve months with hard labour.

The years from 1870–1900 gradually allowed Sheffield women, through legislation, the freedom to live their own lives. Although the crime of wife beating still persists into our modern day, we now have more support for abused wives to get away from the men who were violent towards them. It was not until campaigning by women's groups in the 1970s, resulting in the Domestic Violence and Matrimonial Proceedings Act, that women finally obtained legal protection against abusive husbands. Ordinary women were still powerless, and perhaps nothing epitomises the powerlessness of women under male authority more than that of criminal women caught up in the British legal system.

CHAPTER TWO

Criminal Women and the Justice System

For the years 1850–1950 any woman committing any kind of offence in Sheffield would be taken to the cells underneath the Town Hall, before being brought up before the magistrates the following morning. There she would find that all the arresting officers, as well as the magistrates, solicitors and the clerk of the court were male. It would be a very frightening experience as even on ordinary days the bench would include men of a much higher social rank, with the title of 'esquire' as well as the Mayor of Sheffield. If it was a minor offence and the woman was sentenced, she would be sent to prison where again all the prison officers were male. For any criminal, male or female sent before the Sheffield Quarter Sessions, this would be an even more daunting process, as the bench included two of the most prominent upper-class gentlemen of the area. The Earl of Effingham, Kenneth Alexander Howard, a local landowner, regularly attended, as did his son the Hon. and Rev. William Howard, Rector of Whiston.

Newspapers reveal that in Sheffield one of the most common petty crimes committed by women was usually that of stealing, but what was rarely taken into account, or used in mitigating circumstances, was the fact that many of the perpetrators stole out of pure desperation. One such case heard by the Earl of Effingham on 25 February 1850 was that of a 31-year-old female called Sarah Wigfall who was described as being 'a respectably

Prison-cell windows from the outside of Sheffield Town Hall.

dressed young woman, with a child in her arms'. She was brought before the bench charged with stealing thirty pounds of beef. A Shalesmoor butcher, Mr. F. Dodgson gave evidence that he had been attending to his customers the previous Saturday night, when he saw the girl looking at some pieces of beef in the window. On turning around he noted that a large piece of beef had gone and saw her walking away from the shop and entering a passage at the side of the premises. He followed her and saw her place the meat on the ground and return to where he caught her at the entrance to the passage. No evidence was given into the woman's circumstances or why she had stolen the meat, so the magistrates quickly found her guilty. The Earl of Effingham sentenced her to one month imprisonment with hard labour at Wakefield prison. Depending on the age of the child it would probably have accompanied its mother into prison, with little regard as to its own fate.

For those caught up in more serious crimes they would be sent to take their trial before a high court judge at the assizes, where, once again, the woman would have to stand in the dock surrounded by the men who would make the most important decisions on her life. The circuit or high court judges were treated like gods as they attended the various assizes to hear cases. For example, when Mr Baron Wilde attended the Yorkshire Summer Assizes in York on 9 July 1861, he was attended to with all the pomp and ceremony usually afforded only to royalty. His entry into the city was a carefully orchestrated ritual, attended by heralds and men holding javelins. These displays were purposely made spectacular, to reinforce the authority of the law on people who watched the procession. On the day of the assizes the judge would again be ceremoniously escorted to York Castle to commence his duties by the High Sheriff of Yorkshire, his chaplain, the Under Sheriff and other legal and civic officials. He would then meet with the grand jury and discuss the cases which were due to be heard in front of them the next day, before being driven in state to attend divine service. The grand jury of the assizes courts were all from the most elevated ranks of Yorkshire gentlemen. Although in effect the jury decided on the fate of the prisoner, the high court judge had the power to state what he felt the outcome should be, or he might put pressure onto the members of the jury if he thought their decision was wrong.

One case of the murder of a Sheffield husband by his wife was brought before judge Mr Justice Byles on 5 December 1870. The woman, Charlotte Barton aged somewhere in her fifties, who was also known as Pagden, had attacked her husband Thomas aged 60 years with a hammer at their house on Suffolk Lane on 30 November. The crime of husband murder was taken very seriously by the Victorian legal authorities. Before 1790, women charged with the crime were convicted of 'petit treason' punishable by being burned at the stake, as the definition of the crime was 'the killing of a superior by a subordinate'. Thankfully this horrendous punishment for women was abolished in 1825. Charlotte Barton was found guilty by the Sheffield coroner, John Webster on the following day and she was sent to take her trial at Leeds Assizes. When she appeared before Mr Justice Byles the jury heard that for many years the Sheffield couple had lived very unhappily together, and several

Leeds Town Hall where the Assizes were held.

times Thomas Pagden had tried to make his wife have sex with other men for money, which she refused to do. Neighbours gave evidence as to his unkindness to her, and the prisoner stated that he had provoked her to such an extent that she had hit him on the cellar steps with a hammer. Realising immediately that she was in serious trouble, the prisoner immediately told her brother, who took her to the police station where she confessed to her crime. After hearing all the witnesses the judge directed the jury stating that because she had admitted what she had done, they had to decide what frame of mind she had been in at the time. Thankfully because of the provocation they found her guilty but insane, and she was kept in prison until Her Majesty's pleasure was known.

Charlotte Barton was one of the lucky ones, even though she would spend many years behind bars. But one of the most terrible crimes committed by some single unmarried women were the ones who usually appeared most before the assizes charged with infanticide. These were the women who found themselves pregnant and alone, with no recourse to law. The Poor Law Act of 1834 had absolved the father of all blame, putting the onus on the woman to prove the putative father was the one who had impregnated her. It was widely felt at that time that the responsibility of any pregnancy was clearly the fault of the woman for giving way to her basic feelings. Therefore those women who found themselves in such a condition had little alternative but to free themselves of the 'problem' in what ever way they saw fit. Some faced up to the condemnation and criticism for having a bastard child and reluctantly entered the workhouse, but even among the paupers there, they were treated with the utmost contempt. The conditions within the workhouse and even the limited medical understanding resulted in an incredibly high death rate for all workhouse infants. From the time of the birth of an illegitimate child the mother would be shunned by society, and the child would be labelled a 'bastard' for the remainder of its life. Many took what must have been the most appalling way out of their difficulties and simply abandoned the child on the streets after giving birth, in order to keep their position and their character secret. As a consequence on the streets of Sheffield were found many, many bodies of abandoned newly-born babies, some with horrific injuries.

One of these was the body of a female child which was found on 7 February 1850, with its brains bashed in, by three boys playing in an old abandoned gas tank in Shude Hill, Sheffield. The coroner guessed that the child had been born alive, but killed immediately and the jury returned an open verdict. The finding of these little bodies became so common that when yet another one was found in Old Park Wood on 1 November 1851, an inquest was held, but the coroner knew that the chances of finding the mother were very small. Therefore the only verdict that he could advise the jury to bring in once again was an open verdict. He told them that, 'the body of the child whether male or female could not be ascertained, in consequence of its decomposed state; and how such child came by its death, no evidence could be deduced by the jury'.

A few weeks later, the trunk of another baby's body was found in the remains of an ash pit, from which the head, arms and legs had been removed in order to prevent identification. Once again the jury returned an open verdict. At the time there was little consideration or sympathy for the emotional ordeal gone through by such women as they tried to cover up their 'sin', or little understanding of what drove them to commit such terrible acts after giving birth. When yet another child was found in April 1853 the surgeon gave evidence to say that the child had been born alive and had breathed, however, due to the fact that there were no signs of injury on the body, the only conclusion that he could come to was that the child had died of exposure. The coroner expressed his opinion that the crime of infanticide was on the increase in Sheffield, and he expressed the hope that the 'unnatural mothers' of such infants might be discovered and punished. In one case where the 18-year-old mother was identified to be Maria Woodall she was shown some sympathy, probably because of her youth. The reporter described her as being 'a good looking girl', nevertheless the crime itself was described as so horrible that the evidence was unfit for publication in any detail. The little body had been found in her box at the prisoner's sister's house on Bright Street, Ecclesall Bierlow on 27 March 1850 with a black ribbon wrapped tightly around its neck. Her mother had accused Maria of being pregnant, but upon taking her to a quack who proclaimed himself a professional water caster (an outdated role that is no longer in use), he informed her mother that she was not pregnant, but suffering from dropsy. Upon the child being discovered, Maria was so hysterical that she appeared almost insane. She stated that the father had been an assistant to the chemist, where she had been a domestic servant. On hearing that Maria was pregnant he quickly left his position. When the girl appeared before the Sheffield magistrates, it was reported that she 'appeared so greatly distressed on account of her fearful position that she swooned away several times during the proceedings'. Because of her confession the Sheffield magistrates sent Maria to take her trial at the assizes.

When she was brought before the judge, Mr Justice Cresswell and the grand jury at the York Assizes on 16 July 1850 she pleaded not guilty to the charge of infanticide. The prosecution announced that the grand jury had found no true bill, and therefore she would be tried on the lesser crime of concealment of birth. She was sentenced to a term of imprisonment for twelve months. No doubt Maria was greatly relieved to have been given this lighter sentence, but she would have been very aware that following her prison sentence, she would have been shunned by respectable citizens of Sheffield. Nevertheless she was luckier than another local resident, Mary Thorpe, who was aged 21 and had murdered her child in December 1799 and

Women's Prison at York where Maria Woodall was kept before her trial.

JAMES MILNES, Esquire, High-Sheriff.

MARY Thorpe,	—	—— Guilty, Murder, to be *hanged* on Monday the 17th Day of March, instant and her Body to be afterwards diffected and anatomized.
Michael Simpfon,	——	— Guilty, Murder, to be *hanged* on Monday the 17th Day of March, instant and his Body to be afterwards diffected and anatomized.
Sarah Bailey,	—	—— Guilty, Forgery, *To be hanged.* on the 12 of
John Mac Williams,	——	— Guilty, Forgery, *To be hanged.*
Luke Lee,	—	—— Guilty, Forgery.
William Dalrymple,	—	—— Guilty, Grand Larceny without the Benefit of the Statute, *To be hanged.*
William Sneed,	——	— Guilty, Grand Larceny without the Benefit of the Statute.
Miles Barraclough,	—	—— Guilty, Horfe Stealing.
John Watfon,	——	— Guilty, Horfe Stealing.
George Robinfon,	—	—— Guilty, Horfe Stealing.
Henry Hirft,	——	— Guilty, Sheep Stealing.
Jofeph Walker,	—	—— Guilty, Sheep Stealing.
Richard Booth,	—	— Guilty at the laft Affizes, held for the faid County, of feloniously uttering a Counterfeit Half Crown, having been before convicted of being a common utterer of falfe Money, and Judgment refpited, from Time to Time until the prefent Affizes.

Calendar of Felons 1800 where Mary Thorpe was sentenced to death.

had been brought to trial in March 1800. It was reported that Mary had left her lodgings in the town carrying the baby, and told her landlady that she was taking him to her sister in Derby who would wet-nurse him. Instead she wrapped tape around his neck and killed him by throwing the little body into the river. Found guilty, Mary was hanged at Knavesmire Tyburn, near York and afterwards her body was handed over to surgeons for dissection.

As we have seen, the fates of Charlotte Barton, Maria Woodall and Mary Thorpe would all have been in the hands of men. Thankfully by 1900 there was a small concession in the position of women in the criminal system, when a Sheffield woman, Miss Annie Whaley, was appointed to the Sheffield Police Charge Office. Although her duties were mainly clerical, she would have dealt with female prisoners in their cells. In 1906 she was appointed as a wardress to take care of the female prisoners. Miss Whaley continued in the post until her retirement in 1930 at the age of 70. She told a reporter at the time that she thought that female prisoners in Sheffield were of a 'much rougher character than they had been previously' as she recounted the only time she had been attacked in her job. She had gone to the cells in the Town Hall with a midnight meal of some bread and tea for a prisoner, when she was overpowered

Prisoners were held in cells under the Town Hall, Sheffield as it is today.

by a drunken woman who had been arrested. There being no alarm bell Miss Whaley called for help, but thankfully when her male colleagues arrived the incident was already over. Instead they found her calmly straightening her skirts, whilst the female prisoner equally calmly ate her bread with relish, washing it down with her tea ration. Miss Whaley stated that many of the Sheffield female prisoners that were arrested whilst she was a wardress, were generally charged with drunkenness or sleeping out. Gradually female prisoners could now see one or two women employed in the legal system, as by 1925 it was noted that there were now four female warders in the police cells.

Many philanthropists of Sheffield recognised the link between the committing of crimes by women, and the abundant supply of alcohol in the city's many pubs and beer houses. The Women's Christian Temperance Association were one of the first to concern themselves about the subjection of female prisoners, and decided to employ a woman in 1876 called a court missionary. Initially her role would be to attend the courts and hand out tracts and bibles to women charged as drunkards, prostitutes or other criminals. She also regularly attended court helping women and girls who had been found wandering the streets. The scheme was very successful as magistrates welcomed the calming effect that these women had on the prisoners in the dock.

On 14 May 1887 the wife of one of the local philanthropists, Mrs Henry J. Wilson, inserted an advertisement in the local newspaper requesting a Christian woman over the age of 30 years, who had to be a total abstainer from alcohol, for the position of Church Missionary. By November of the same year they were able to appoint a second woman, who was now called Lady Missionary Agent. Now women prisoners brought before the magistrates could be referred to the court missionary as an alternative to being given a custodial sentence, and they became very much the forerunners of our present day Probation Service. Their duties had widened to the point where they visited the offender at home or, in the case of those who were actually convicted, waited outside the prison gates after they had finished their sentence. The court missionaries had no legal powers, apart from offering good advice and support and helping prisoners to return back to a respectable life. By this time they worked with men, women and children. Sometimes assistance was given in the form of clothing, food, or tools, or they could speak to a former employer to ask them to take back the prisoner into their previous position, particularly if they were known to the magistrates to be of good character. Later that year the work of the court missionary had proved to be so popular in Sheffield that, despite the fact that other organisations had recruited women for the same role, the demand could not keep up with the supply.

On 19 December 1887 a case was brought before the Sheffield magistrates involving a robbery by a domestic servant called Rose Amy Worthington. She had been charged with stealing a jacket belonging to her mistress Mrs Varley of Havelock Square, Sheffield, and had been remanded into the custody of

Paradise Square as it is today.

her father. She then refused to go home with him, but she did agree to go with another court missionary, Miss Thompson from the House of Help in Paradise Square. Sadly the home was so overcrowded that Miss Thompson told the court that they were unable to take her on at that time. All the other court missionaries were also busy, so the magistrates had no option but to set Rose at liberty, on her writing out a promise that she would not offend again. It was hoped that she would be assigned one of the missionaries when one became available.

On 14 September 1900 another Sheffield woman called Maud Collinson aged 19, was brought into the court charged with two cases of obtaining money by false pretences. The girl claimed that she was a nurse and was fraudulently obtaining subscriptions from people in the street, which she stated was to be given to the nurses' home. In fact she was still wearing a nurse's uniform when she was brought before the bench. It seems that Maud had run away from home and was making a living for herself by these 'subscriptions'. She was sentenced to prison for one month with hard labour, and the magistrate requested that when she came out of prison a court missionary would be assigned to her.

In the *Sheffield Independent* of 20 November 1917 one of these early missionaries, a Miss Robinson, was interviewed and she gave the reporter her opinion of the Sheffield women who were brought before the magistrates. She stated that:

> every girl or woman convicted is not inherently vicious, but many are not vigorous mentally and therefore they need safeguarding and guidance. Many men and boys have been given the chance to redeem their characters by serving in the Great War, and the same opportunity should be given to many girls and women who have committed small crimes. Whilst some may be steered towards munitions work, many others take different paths, and it is here where the court missionary can help. When women come out of prison they require direction as to their future path, and someone to take an interest in her. The women court missionaries are able to arrange to help when their sentence has been served.

Miss Robinson told the reporter that they also work with children charged with crimes who come from homes where parental control is weak, owing to poverty or intemperance. She concluded that Sheffield mothers who are habitually underfed have not the physical or mental stamina needed to bring up their families with wise discipline, and so the children promptly get out of hand and into mischief. Miss Robinson said that many of them may find themselves put on probation and that's when the court missionaries offer support. They stay in touch with the young person by using their personal interest and influence, thereby preventing them from falling into crime again. She admitted that whilst they are not successful in every case, there were enough successes to make the role worthwhile. Miss Robinson then told the reporter about one of her cases she had taken on a short while previously. She had received a letter asking her to visit a mother of a large family who had been left a widow in straitened circumstances. The woman had four boys under the age of 12 who were constantly getting into trouble, as well as other younger children. The mother told her that 'they simply cheek me and I cannot do anything with them'. Because of the younger children she was unable to work herself and supplement the small allowance she had as a widow, which was not enough to keep them all adequately nourished. She had been in despair until someone mentioned the Sheffield Court Missionary Service to her where she had requested some help. Taking an action, which would not be recommended today, the four younger boys had subsequently been sent to a Working Boys Home. However, this did give the widow an ability to care for the other children much better. Miss Robinson said that her role had involved much running around and letter writing, as well as attendance at the police court. For those women who wished to follow her example and become court missionaries, she advocated that they must be deeply sympathetic, but not sentimental. Their powers of discernment must be widely developed, and they must never forget to be constantly on the alert.

It is not known when professional female probation officers were employed in the Sheffield police courts, but by February 1925 they were said to be 'doing most splendid work'. But the Police Court Missionaries employed by the Sheffield Temperance Association would seem to be working alongside the paid probation officers in May 1930, although it appears that their focus was mainly to redeem prisoners from their dependence on alcohol. In May 1932 a report on the work of the Police Court Missionaries was given by magistrate Dr Helen Wilson. She stated that out of 500 men, women and children who were brought into the Sheffield Court, 328 had eventually signed the pledge. Dr Wilson said that twenty years previously it was not unusual to have ten women in the Sheffield police cells charged with offences of drunkenness on Monday mornings. However, she stated that 'today such a charge against a woman was rare'.

By the 1920s women were now employed in the prison office and missionaries in the courts, but what took more time to achieve was to actually get a woman on the bench of magistrates in Sheffield. It was particularly distressing for those females who were victims of sexual abuse, having to give evidence in a courtroom full of men, and therefore it was felt very strongly that women magistrates should be appointed to deal with those kinds of cases. In October 1919 the *Sheffield Independent* also questioned why Sheffield had no female magistrates on the bench. The article stated that there were now such women magistrates in America, Australia and Canada and commented that 'for men only to sit in judgement on a woman is a crime in itself'. The report noted that in Sheffield alone, every year there were over 2,000 women and girls brought before male magistrates, charged with different offences. The reporter also ruefully noted that most male magistrates were appointed as a reward for long service in the public interest, or because that man had been a supporter in cash to a particular political party. He concluded:

> In history therefore it had always been a close preserve for pompous, middle-class gentlemen, not always too well endowed with brains. How can charges against women be fair, when the whole procedure of a police court is under masculine control?

It was not until the passing of the Sex Disqualification (Removal) Act in 1920 that finally ensured that no woman should be disqualified from holding any position or office purely on account of her sex. The Lord Chancellor had no option but to agree, and he formed a committee who recommended local women for the post of magistrate. As a result of this it was announced in July 1920 that three Sheffield women were appointed on the basis of their public activities and not for their affiliation to political parties. The three women were; Mrs Frances Stephenson of Banner Cross Hall, Dr Helen Wilson of Osgathorpe Hills and Mrs Eleanor Barton of Stannington Road Malin Bridge. The three women took the oath of allegiance before the mayor, Councillor S. Roberts a few days later. It was announced that these women had been appointed 'having all rendered themselves conspicuous by distinguished public service'. Dr Helen Wilson had long been active in Sheffield being on the Committee of the Association for Moral and Social Hygiene. Mrs Stephenson had twice been Lady Mayoress and Mistress Cutler of Sheffield and chair of the women's hostel at the university. Mrs Barton was the Vice Chair of the National Women's Co-operative Guild, as well as being a member of the Housing and Maternity and Child Welfare committees. Several other local women were elected magistrates over the next few years, and by 1928 there were fifteen female Sheffield magistrates. Nevertheless, despite their elevation, women magistrates figured largely in the juvenile courts rather than in the police courts.

Another impact that the Sex Disqualification Act had on the Sheffield courts was that women were now able to sit on a jury. Historically women had only served on special juries before when a panel of matrons was required. These had to be empanelled if a woman, found guilty of a serious crime, claimed to be pregnant. The women appointed to sit on such a jury were not required to decide the prisoner's guilt or not, just to swear as to whether she was pregnant. Many women found guilty of murder claimed this privilege in order to delay the execution, however, these special juries fell out of use as fewer women were executed. Following the implementation of the Act, Sheffield women could now sit in court with male jurors, listen to all the evidence and reach a verdict of guilty or not guilty. The *Sheffield Independent* noted on 16 October 1920 that women jurors had sat for the very first time in the Sheffield Quarter Sessions the previous morning. It was such a novelty that although the Court Recorder initially correctly addressed the court by 'Ladies and Gentlemen', as time went on he lapsed into the more familiar 'gentlemen' at one point. There had been much opposition nationally to the appointment of female jurors, as it was felt that women lacked the mental capacity to listen to the sometimes gruesome evidence. This opinion was clarified by the National Union of Equal Citizenships who told a *Sheffield Independent* reporter on 3 May 1921 that:

- All married women whose husbands are qualified for jury service shall be similarly liable.
- That no judge, or chairman of quarter sessions, can claim that a case should be heard without women jurors, if a child or woman is concerned in the case, either as prisoner or witness.
- In a criminal action, neither the accused nor the prosecution may raise an objection to women jurors on account of their sex.

It is impossible to calculate how many Sheffield women served on juries, but throughout the 1920s more and more women were seen in the courtrooms. The first solicitor to appear in any Yorkshire Police Court was Miss Mary Sykes of Huddersfield in March 1923. But it was not until December 1927 when the first woman solicitor appeared, not in Sheffield but in the Rotherham Police Court, although her mother, Mrs J.E. Taylor of Shiregreen was a Sheffield woman. At the time her daughter Mrs Mary Brittain lived in Rotherham where she had been articled to her brother-in-law, Mr L.H. Brittain for five years. The mayor of Rotherham Councillor W. Brooks in his capacity as magistrate, greeted her saying 'it is the first time I have had the opportunity of welcoming you to this court, and I hope your career will be a successful one'. In July 1929 Mrs Brittain finally appeared in the Sheffield Police Court where, showing a sympathy missing in many of the male solicitors of the time, she succeeded in getting just a fine for her client Mrs Gladys Wilson. The 31 year old was fined 40s for stealing clothes, instead of a custodial sentence. Mrs Brittain had argued successfully that her client had nine children, eight of whom were under the age of 11 and the youngest only three weeks old. She pointed out to the male members of the bench that if they sentenced Mrs Wilson to prison, the youngest child would have to accompany her. She concluded that 'it is rather a terrible thing to think of that child practically starting its life in prison'. The magistrates agreed and instead the woman was fined.

Eventually the appearance of professional women in court became so common that it was rarely mentioned in the local newspapers, but there is little doubt that there had been much opposition to women entering the legal professions which had previously been closed to them. It took persistent campaigning by women's groups throughout the 1930s, 1940s and 1950s before they were fully accepted. But it is because of them that we now have more sympathetic treatment of women and girls in court, particularly those involved in distressing rape or sexual abuse cases.

It was during the Victorian period that the ideology of the role of a woman became more refined and rigid. The polarity of the image of pure women as the 'angel of the home' against the whores known as the 'fallen women' were the way in which many men saw women of the time. Respectable women were expected to stay chaste until marriage and only to have conversations with men accompanied by a chaperone. Fallen women were usually working-class females who serviced the needs of men in exchange for cash. Only when the rapid increase of syphilis became so prevalent that it was called the great social evil, was the government forced to do something about it. Needless to say when the all-male Parliament brought in the Contagious Diseases Acts of 1864, 1866 and 1869, it galvanised a major feminist movement whose effects stretched to Sheffield and other towns and cities of the West Riding.

CHAPTER THREE

Sex, Prostitution and the Contagious Diseases Acts

As we have already seen, many women saw marriage as their only respectable future and must therefore have experienced a great sense of achievement when a man proposed marriage, and the couple became engaged. The idea of marriage itself was seen as a contract, and if that contract was broken she could sue the man for breach of promise. Many men saw the engagement itself as a prelude to illicit sexual relations and if the girl became pregnant and he refused to marry her, she had little recourse to law. The only way in which a seducer could be challenged, was by the girl taking the man to court and having a jury assess damages for the loss of her reputation. However, this exposed the girl to having her most private details discussed in open court. In order to prove a case intimate letters would often be read out, which naturally became a source of gossip in the local newspapers. In the dual standards common in Victorian society, one person might see that the girl was now 'ruined' and that no respectable man would marry her, or another that the damages she received might be seen as a potential dowry for some unscrupulous fortune hunter.

On 27 October 1871 such a local case was heard in the Sheriffs Court at York Castle when Miss Sarah Jane Dickenson, aged 25, accused William Bramall, aged 24, of declining to fulfil his promise to marry her. The court was told that Miss Dickenson came from a respectable Sheffield family, and had been a music teacher with seven pupils, which earned her a living of £20 a year.

She lived at Oughtibridge with her parents and was described as an 'inexperienced girl' when she was seduced by Bramall, and as a result had given birth at the age of only 19 years. She had met him in 1868 and he had paid court to her as an engaged couple, which was accepted by her family. The couple planned to marry at Ecclesfield Church, Sheffield in December of 1869. When Bramall informed her that as his fiancée he required her to give up her pupils, she immediately agreed. Despite this, as the time for the wedding arrived, the reluctant bridegroom made some excuse and the wedding was re-organised for 1 February 1870, although as the time approached, he claimed that they would once again have to postpone the ceremony. In order to placate his future bride on 25 March 1870 the couple went into Sheffield where he bought her a diamond engagement ring and the couple set another date for 17 May.

No doubt as a result of the security of a ring on her finger, Miss Dickenson foolishly 'yielded to his advances' and on 10 May 1871 she gave birth to a fine baby boy. When her father challenged Mr Bramall as to why he had not married his daughter, he said that he fully intended to make her his wife, declaring that 'he could not live without her and the baby'. A new wedding date was set for two months later in June, but on the Friday before the set date, Bramall went to see his fiancée and told her that not only would he not marry her, but that he doubted the child was his. Mr Dickenson went to see a solicitor and a letter was sent to Bramall suggesting a sum of compensation for damages, which he refused to pay. After hearing all the evidence, the jury was instructed by the judge to assess the damages to be awarded to Miss Dickenson. Mr Bramall's defence counsel, Mr Blackburn, urged the jury to be liberal in the amount of compensation they awarded in view of the young man's limited earnings. He stated that his client was living with his father and therefore was not in possession of a great fortune. He pointed out that Mr Bramall had agreed to pay some damages, although the sum was not found to be acceptable by Mr Dickenson. He referred to the fact that Miss Dickenson had given birth to a child at the early age of 19 and audaciously claimed:

that her misfortune at that time had not taught her a lesson, as she had gained no experience from her yielding in the first instance. Therefore to give heavy damages, under such circumstances, would only be a premium to vice.

To add insult to injury, when Mr Bramall was called to give evidence he agreed that he had promised to marry Miss Dickenson, yet he still claimed in court that the child was not his. The room was then cleared and the jury deliberated before giving a verdict that Mr Bramall must pay damages of £150, a substantial sum for the time.

Inevitably some women were taken advantage of without the promise of marriage, and they had no recourse to law themselves only through the girl's father. Many seduction cases came before the judge at the assizes, and once again the hearing of the details was in itself a very traumatic experience for both parties. Such a case from Sheffield was brought before the Yorkshire Assizes on 8 March 1852 where the local newspaper described the unfairness of the legal process. It declared:

this was one of those sad cases in which a father and daughter were compelled to come into court, and expose to public gaze the disgrace suffered by the one and the shame brought upon the other, in order to obtain from the hands of a jury what is nominally called compensation in damages. In reality, however, it is in fact much more frequently for the purpose of inflicting on the defendant the wrongdoer and seducer in the shape of damages, the only punishment which the law in its wisdom had yet thought proper to impose upon criminals of this description.

The case was of a girl called Miss Macnolty who was described as being 'in humble life' whilst the seducer was an older married man called Mason, who carried on the business of plumber and glazier at Snig Hill, Sheffield. He had employed her in October

Snig Hill as it is today.

1850 when she was only 15 years of age, to work in his shop. Mason and his wife were well known to the Macnolty family, who lived adjacent to his shop at Snig Hill, so they accordingly gave their blessings for her to enter his service. About Christmas time he seduced her and the intercourse lasted for some months, until noting that she was pregnant, Mason discharged her in a very harsh way without any warning. On 20 December 1851 the girl gave birth, but when he was approached for maintenance for the child, Mason denied all knowledge of it. At the assizes the judge, Baron Alderson stated that having heard all the evidence, he could only deduce that the man had taken the girl into his service with the sole aim of seducing her. Her father made a small living as a musician; nevertheless, he told the jury, he was a man who suffered as deeply from the seduction of his child as those in a much higher station in life. The judge asked them to award such damages which might constitute a fair, reasonable and adequate compensation for the injury that Mr Macnolty had sustained. The jury awarded damages of £60 to be paid to him.

Although it is well known that Queen Victoria refused to acknowledge such a thing as lesbianism, it did exist, and an early case in Sheffield in 1860 indicated that it was acknowledged and recognised. If a man deserted his wife, who he was bound to support, then she had no option but to go on parish relief or enter the workhouse. Consequently he could then be charged and brought to court in order to pay his wife's maintenance. On 2 April Henry Whittington of Sheffield was brought before the magistrates' court charged with a refusal to maintain his wife, and the court was told that it was not the first time he had been charged with deserting her. His defence solicitor, Mr Maule claimed that although the Sheffield magistrates had previously imposed an order to pay to his wife, he was appealing against it. He called witnesses to prove that his wife was living in adultery with another woman. Mr West, Mrs Whittington's own solicitor, told the magistrates that she had been bound to leave him through his own cruelty. Mr Maule claimed that the appeal was made due to his wife's adultery and therefore he should, under the law of the land, not be liable for her maintenance. The magistrates agreed and the previous conviction was quashed.

Given the limited opportunities for respectable employment for a woman in a town like Sheffield, it was inevitable that many of them had no option but to turn to prostitution for a living. Nevertheless it was believed by many in the Victorian period that women who were prostitutes took to it simply due to their own profligacy, idleness or love of vice. The sad reality was that in many circumstances it was the only way for many local women to earn a living. If a woman had lost her respectability, having been abandoned by a husband or partner, or had served a term of imprisonment her working potential was lessened, and if she had any children it was doubly so. It is not surprising therefore that many women turned to the age-old role. It was a double-edged sword as once entering into the world of prostitution, it was very difficult to leave, as such a profession ensured a woman would now be seen as a hardened criminal and she would never be able to get respectable employment again. The seriousness of the number of prostitutes in the town had been brought to the attention of the Sheffield Police Commissioners in 1842. An inspector for children employed in the factories, Mr. J.C. Symons told the chief constable that 'the state of morals in Sheffield was worse than in any other town'. When asked how many such women made a living through prostitution, the chief constable stated that it was difficult to judge as during times of economic depression many married women took up the trade temporarily just to make ends meet. The commissioners discussed how the problem could be eradicated, but the chief constable told them that it was impossible as when such women were charged, the only thing they could do was to send them to prison at Wakefield for a month. However, not only was that a considerable expense to the town to do so, but the women came back no better behaved, but were hardened prostitutes having mixed with others much worse than themselves. The view of Sheffield legal authorities was that these women were a blight on the more respectable citizens of the town, and simply existed just to separate men from their hard-earned wages.

The realities of the hardships of such a life were brought to the attention of the local people in September 1854, following an inquest held on a woman who had openly lived for many years as a prostitute. The conditions in which she had lived shocked the members of the jury after they visited the deceased at the house at West Court, Sheffield. The body of the poor woman still lay on the bed where it had been found. The *Sheffield and Rotherham Independent* described the surroundings:

> the hovel (for it was nothing else) in which the body lay, had formerly been let off as two dwellings, that on the ground floor being occupied by the deceased and the upper portion, to which there was an entrance on the outside by a flight of stone steps, by others of the same class. Latterly in consequence of its dilapidated state, it had been used for storing old fish hampers. The roof was in such a state as to afford no protection against the weather, and the walls were built of nothing but laths and plaster. The plaster which had fallen off, left nothing

but the bare laths, through which both the wind and rain found its way. The hovel in which the body lay, was not in any part more than five or six feet wide, and so small that only a portion of the jury could be admitted at one time. There was only an old rotten bed on which she lay, and a broken chair and table. The bed had only a filthy quilt for covering, and the walls were in the most filthy state [...] On one side of the room were two small windows in which nearly every square of glass had been broken and some of the holes stopped up with rags.

The Sheffield prostitutes who claimed the most sympathy from society were those who had been lured into the work at a very young age. In 1862 the age of sexual consent in Britain for young girls was 12 years, and a case which was brought before the Sheffield bench in February 1862 was described as 'one of the worst cases of depravity that ever shocked a court of justice'. The court was told how two young girls, Ellen Walsh of Pea Croft and Mary Clarke of Water Lane had accosted a young man from Birmingham named William Thompson on 5 February 1862. He had been walking along Bridge Street, Sheffield when they approached him and asked him if he wanted to go with them. They took him to a house in Newhall Street and he went upstairs with the younger prisoner. On coming back downstairs he found that £6 in gold and silver had been stolen from his purse, and he reported the matter to the police. The next morning the two girls were both brought into court. The young girl Walsh appeared first and there was an audible shock as she was placed in the dock. It was noted that she was so small for her age that she could barely see over the sides of the dock into the body of the court. One of the magistrates asked her how old she was and she told them she was 12 years of age. As a consequence it was reported that:

This caused the greatest disgust in the minds of the bench and nearly all present in the courtroom. The statement that such a little girl had voluntarily prostituted herself when she was so young, appeared almost incredible to the bench.

Walsh's mother, who was waiting in the entrance hall, was sent for and when asked her daughter's age said that she was 11 years the previous August, to which there was the greatest consternation in the courtroom. However, Mrs Walsh was probably being disingenuous, as she knew full well that if the girl had been found to be only 11 years of age, the blame would be placed squarely on the shoulders of the man William Thompson. At this point the prisoner told the court that 'she told me she was 14'. Hearing this, Mrs Walsh turned around in court and struck her daughter violently across the face with her clenched fist. Thompson, in an attempt to recover himself, admitted that he had been drunk at the time he had gone with the two girls. Mr A. Smith, the prosecutor stated that instead of blaming the girl, it was he that was punishable, notwithstanding the circumstances under which he had met her in the street. The bench agreed that Thompson should be remanded until further information could be obtained about the girl, and it was reported that the man himself seemed stunned at the turn of events as he left the room.

Thompson and the two girls were brought back into court on 8 February 1862 when once again it was reported that the repetition of the details of the case caused the greatest disgust in court. The magistrate, Mr Dunn told them that he felt:

> indignant that a man should avail himself of the offer of a mere child willing to prostitute herself. If a child was precocious in harlotry, she was not to be made use of by a drunken, debauched, and worthless fellow.

The chief constable told the court that he had made enquiries and had ascertained from the Roman Catholic Church in Liverpool, where the girl had been baptised, that she was in fact 14 years of age. At this the bench gave orders that the girl was to be remanded at large, whilst arrangements were made to send her to a reformatory. The magistrates also decided that as there was no corroboration to Thompson's statement that he had been robbed, he would therefore be discharged. The magistrate's clerk told a local reporter that 'he was left to his own reflections, which could not be very pleasant ones'. The reporter gleefully reminded readers that 'Thompson was a married man and therefore the reflections which doubtless awaited him at home will be of a very unpleasant character, when the history of his short, but disastrous visit to Sheffield is made known.'

The age of consent was only raised to 13 years in an amendment to the Offences against the Person Act of 1875 and was later raised to 16 years in the Criminal Law Amendment Act of 1885.

The way in which some young innocent girls were lured into a life of prostitution in Sheffield was highlighted in January 1857 when a girl gave her evidence in court. A man called Samuel Cole and his wife had been charged with running a bawdy house, but the evidence showed that the couple hired girls to work as live-in domestic servants at the public house, but then forced them to sleep with men. One of the girls named Harriet Bramhall told the magistrates that she had gone into domestic service with the couple where she worked for just three days. She was taken aback when Mrs Cole and her husband Samuel ordered her to sleep with a man for money on the second night, and she refused. Mrs Cole told her that she did not want a domestic servant and would not pay to keep her, and consequently the following day she left. Harriet told the court that whilst she was at the house, there had been another girl who was also employed as a domestic servant. On two of the three nights the poor girl had been persuaded to sleep with men with the full knowledge and connivance of Mr and Mrs Cole. Samuel Cole was defended in court by solicitor Mr Broadbent whose cross examination of Harriet, rather than defend his client, made clear just exactly what the house was being used for. In a startling turn of events, her answers so disgusted Mr Broadbent, that he told his client that he could defend himself before leaving the court. The girl's mother, Mrs Bramhall and her aunt also gave evidence that when they heard her story, they went to the house a few nights after her daughter had returned home. Mrs Bramhall told the magistrates that they wanted to see for themselves exactly what kind of a house it was, and to make sure that Harriet was telling the truth. She told the court that they observed 'some men in a room with five women who were conducting themselves in a very immodest manner'. The prisoner, Mr Cole, stated that this was a complete fabrication and the only woman in the house that night had been one who had come to fetch some beer for her husband. The magistrates disagreed and they fined him £3 with 8s costs.

Another similar case was heard when a female brothel-keeper was brought before the bench on 13 June 1876. Annie Ashton was charged with keeping a 'disorderly house' on Rockingham Street, Sheffield. She had been before the magistrates earlier for the same offence, when she had been warned that next time she would be sent to prison without the option of a fine. One of the young girls she employed gave evidence against her. Mary Colopy told the court that she had only worked for Ashton for three weeks and she admitted to taking men to the house on Rockingham Street, and when they gave her money she had to give it to her employer. Ashton's solicitor boldly stated that the house had not been a 'disorderly' house at all, but claimed that his client had seen that it had been a very well-conducted house. However, he promised the bench that if they simply fined his client he would guarantee that she would move out of Sheffield. Ashton was warned by the magistrates as to what would happen if she was brought in front of them again, and fined the maximum penalty of £10.

There were some respectable Sheffield people who looked on local prostitutes with some sympathy. A letter dated 6 April 1858 from someone signing themselves simply as 'A WOMAN' appeared in the *Sheffield Independent* who thought that some local women and girls needed help rather than condemnation. The writer advocated that an asylum be established in the town to help the girls who wanted to escape from such a dreadful life. She stated that many of Sheffield's philanthropic women were already trying to help those 'unfortunates' whose only escape from that kind of life was to enter the workhouse. Although many of those kind women offered the hand of friendship to such girls, the nearest possible refuge was an establishment in Leeds as there was nothing comparable in Sheffield. The letter stated that 'there are many of these women who would gladly leave their infamous ways, but that they have neither friends, money nor character. In the present state of affairs, who would employ a woman in business without any of these.'

Declaring that the want of such an institution was 'a public disgrace to the citizens of Sheffield' the writer asked that some people join together to establish such a refuge, which could only work for public good. A reply to the letter was written the following week from a correspondent signing himself simply as 'A MAN', which described the town prostitutes as 'fallen, but repentant females' and claimed that the reason why such a place of refuge had not been established already was because it was a case of 'false delicacy' on the part of men. Other sympathetic people agreed. On 17 June 1856 a Mr Joseph Harding, the secretary of the long-winded 'Associate Institution for Improving and Enforcing the Laws for the Protection of Women', delivered a lecture at the Town Hall, Sheffield on the subject. Speaking to an audience which consisted mainly of females, Mr Harding, despite the aims of the Institution for which he worked, declared that men had to be saved from themselves. He stated that the aim of his Society was prevention rather than cure, and that young men who formed acquaintances with such degraded women needed to be protected from themselves. By using the services of these women he would thereby contract expensive and evil habits, and as a result they would find themselves committing such crimes as embezzlement and larceny from their employers, in order to fund their habit. Mr Harding urged local ministers of the town to speak urgently to their congregations and in particular their young people, on the subject, and he also condemned the public houses which harboured such women, claiming that they were as bad as the houses of ill fame which proliferated in the town of Sheffield. He also agreed that the want of such an institution was 'a public disgrace to the citizens of Sheffield'.

On 23 April 1861 Mr Joseph Harding visited the town once again to reiterate his request that a refuge for prostitutes be opened in the town without delay. The meeting, which was held in the Music Hall, was on this occasion attended by a great number of young men. The subject matter was supposed to be of such great importance in Sheffield that the mayor himself took the chair. He told the meeting that a regrettably small committee of women had long been established in the town, in order to help the prostitutes. He stated that through their efforts, they had saved over 260 women and girls, who were now in respectable employment, but the committee's means were small and donations were urgently required for them to be able to continue. The mayor stated that prostitution was a growing concern in Sheffield and in particular 'the great numbers of women and girls in our factories and workshops, who might be subjected to the same temptations under which so many of their sisters had fallen'.

He stated that the concerns about prostitution in Sheffield were increasing as those women who were removed by death and disease, were replaced by 'young, beautiful and beloved women, who had been led away to fill up the horrible gap'. Mr Harding agreed and said that with the provision of a refuge in Sheffield, such women could 'cast off the morbid and criminal shame' and under proper instruction would 'implore Divine mercy for their unhappy sisters'. Rev. J. Burbidge thanked Mr Harding for his eloquent appeal and told the assembly that at that time a house had been offered on Gell Street, Sheffield and a person was willing to become its matron, although funds needed to be collected in order for the idea to take shape. Addressing the audience he pleaded 'would these gentlemen of Sheffield not let these favourable circumstances slip, by withholding the money'. He read a report which confirmed that during the last year twelve former Sheffield prostitutes had found employment in comfortable situations in Leeds, and twenty more had been restored to their friends. Since that time, however, the Leeds Asylum had sent a letter refusing to accept any more unfortunate women from Sheffield, due to their own overcrowding.

Mr Harding's appeal was successful and a Refuge for Penitent Females was opened on Gell Street, Sheffield some time later that year. Unfortunately, due to its reliance on public funds, by 1871 the building was reported to be 'almost in ruins' and once again urgent appeals were being made for funding through local newspapers.

Nevertheless the creation of the 'Sheffield House of Help for Friendless Girls and Young Women' which opened in May 1886 in Paradise Square, Sheffield soon became the desired refuge. Originally designed as an employment agency and emergency lodgings for young women, it soon became the place for girls wishing to escape from their life as a prostitute. In August the local newspaper reported:

> It has not long been in existence, but a three month experience has abundantly satisfied its promoters that it was greatly needed. During that time the number of applicants for admission has averaged 15 a day, their ages being from 14 to 20 and all of them friendless and homeless.

The head matron was a woman called Miss Turner and she requested that all donations of money, furniture or clothing be directed to her. In a similar appeal the honorary secretary, Mrs Phoebe Flather particularly asked for clothing as some of the girls arrived in a dirty and unkempt state. Many affluent Sheffield women were drawn towards helping on the committee for this important work and at a conference held at the Montgomery Hall on 25 January 1888, there were seventeen local women including the Mistress Cutler and Lady Stephenson of Hassop Hall, Derbyshire who were on the platform. At the first annual report held on 22 February 1888 it was stated that the Home had received 1,200 applications for help and that 165 Sheffield girls had passed through the institution, mostly those from 'impure or dangerous surroundings'. They had been sent to respectable institutions for training and re-settlement and three had emigrated. Mrs Flather told the assembled audience

Montgomery Hall, as it was in May 1884.

that to their shame many of these girls had been introduced to
the immoral life by their own mothers, in order to contribute
what they could to the family finances. Mrs Flather explained
that:

> the depravity of daily life of many of the poor in
> Sheffield was not to be wondered at, when many of their
> own workers went into the courts and streets. There they
> saw father and mother, big sons and daughters all living
> in two or three roomed houses where proper sleeping
> accommodation could not be found.

She stated that as the girls entered the Home they were assessed and put into categories for classification. For example a girl that was deemed as having 'lived among immoral people, though not herself having fallen' was still thought to be a dangerous companion for other young girls at the Home seeking employment. It was agreed that such a girl might 'do incalculable harm' if placed among her more respectable peers. It was decided to split those seeking work from those at danger of immorality, and the former would now be placed in the Girls Training Home which was opened in Fawcett Street. The House of Help in Paradise Square would continue to protect and rescue 'young women who have fallen from virtue and desire to redeem their character'. The pioneering work of rescuing prostitutes undertaken by the House of Help was said to be the first ever established in the whole of Great Britain at that time.

Mrs Phoebe Flather was involved in all aspects of the rescue work and continued to visit the local workhouse and hospitals, encouraging many of the fallen girls to come to the House of Help. However, the reality was that many of the girls, used to freedom were unable to settle to working as a poorly-paid domestic servant. One of these was Annie Marie Shaw, aged 19, who had been attended at the police court by one of the missionaries, Mrs Loran. She had nowhere to stay, and had been found wandering the streets and charged with vagrancy. Her mother had died seventeen months previously and since that time the girl had lived on the streets. Annie was brought to the House on 23 July 1891, but it was already overcrowded and, having no beds, they promised her that if she would stay at the workhouse for just a short time they would try to help. Sadly, she discharged herself a few days later and disappeared. Mrs Flather later found her in the lock ward of Fir Vale workhouse hospital where she visited her several times. These wards were specifically designed to treat women suffering from venereal disease. Annie told Mrs Flather that she would come to the House, but once again discharged herself from the hospital wards and disappeared.

Many of the girls were sent to refuges in other parts of the country, in order to get them away from their old haunts in

Sheffield. One such girl was Jane Sanderson who had been living at Gibson's lodging house on the appropriately named Love Lane, Sheffield. She was aged 19 and was described as 'destitute and a fallen girl'. Her only respectable employment had been working with her mother in the fields of a Mrs Stevenson of Seaforth Grange near Bawtry. Her father was described as being too old to work and was therefore dependent on the money earned by his wife and daughter. Despite her employment Jane had no friends to give her a reference in order for her to apply for respectable employment. She had been brought into the House late on the night of 5 April 1888 and had been reported to be 'intoxicated, but quiet'. The House of Help had offered to send her to a refuge in another town, but she refused and left the house two days later.

As we have seen many people were sympathetic to the plight of Sheffield prostitutes, but it was the subject of the Contagious Diseases Acts introduced in 1860s which brought numbers of Sheffield women together to change legislation. Under the provision of these Acts the police had the power to arrest and have examined, forcibly if need be, any woman merely suspected of being a prostitute, using an intrusive object called a speculum. If the woman was found to be suffering from venereal disease, she could be compulsorily confined in a lock hospital for up to three months. The matter which people objected to most, was the fact that when brought before the magistrates the onus was on the woman to prove that she was not a prostitute. At first this intrusive procedure was simply confined to garrison towns, but there was general outcry in 1866 when it was extended to all the towns and cities in the north of England.

The inconsistency between the way in which the two genders were being dealt with infuriated Elizabeth Wolstenholme and Josephine Butler, causing them to band together and form the Ladies National Association for the Repeal of the Contagious Diseases Acts in 1869. Elizabeth Wolstenholme of Manchester was a self-taught woman who strongly believed in improving the quality of women's education. Josephine Butler, the wife of Rev. George Butler, from Liverpool, also felt strongly about women's education and they were both blisteringly critical of the Victorian double standards of the time.

In Sheffield, a local couple, Mr and Mrs Henry Joseph Wilson, also decided to do something about it in September 1870. They had become associated with Josephine Butler, and they invited her to come and talk to the people of Sheffield to ask for their support to ban these Acts. Despite the fact that the subject was judged to be too delicate to be talked about in respectable company, Mrs Butler was greeted with great enthusiasm by the people of the town. It was reported that:

> with undoubted moral courage and singular earnestness Mrs Josephine Butler has imposed upon herself the task of stirring up the English people to demand the repeal of certain Acts, which she denounces as utterly immoral, unconstitutional and abhorrent to every principle and feeling becoming a Christian people.

Mrs Butler was speaking at the Cutlers' Hall, Sheffield when she told her audience that she truly believed that 'God had chosen women to be in the front of this battle', yet even the local newspapers noted with some irony that the rest of the platform consisted only of men. Nevertheless Mrs Butler argued that 'most of the legal Acts of this country applied to both sexes, apart from this one Act'. She stated that as a result of this legislation, any respectable women could be dragged into court and required to prove that she was not a common prostitute. If she was found guilty she was forced to 'have her person outraged by the periodical inspection of a surgeon, over a period of twelve months, or by resisting she would be imprisoned for one to three months'. In her investigations into the subject, Mrs Butler claimed that many women arrested under such a false accusation made by the police, had been so terrified at the idea of a public trial that under intimidation, they had signed away their good name and were then listed wrongly as a prostitute. A further meeting of 'women only' was held at the Cutlers' Hall at noon the following day, where Mrs Butler

Cutlers' Hall, where Josephine Butler spoke in September 1870.

addressed the audience at considerable length and found that she had much support. She described how she had appealed to men to do something to condemn the laws, but had got nowhere. Mrs Butler stated that it was up to the women of Sheffield to do something about this matter and urged all those who supported her to expose the 'iniquity and foulness of the Acts in order to throw light on them'. To resounding cheers she concluded that:

> Sheffield had been but late awakened in the matter, but I have no doubt it would make its voice heard as powerfully as other large towns had done. It is a question both constitutionally and morally which solely affected the working classes and they should wage war to the death against this kind of legislation.

In order to push the matter forward Mrs Butler asked that a resolution be passed from the meeting condemning the Acts, and that a petition to Parliament be delivered by their local MP. Her words encouraged the formation of the Sheffield Ladies Association and a large number of respectable local women enrolled at once. Such was the abhorrence which the people of the country felt against the Acts, that the government was forced to look into the matter and they ordered a report to be prepared. However, in what would pre-empt the frustrations which the suffragettes were later to realise with the government, when the long awaited report was finally submitted to Parliament in July 1871, recommending an immediate repeal of the Acts, nothing was done.

In Sheffield in February 1872, yet another meeting condemning the Contagious Diseases Acts was held in the Temperance Hall, Sheffield, where Rev. Samuel Earnshaw of the Parish Church took the chair, and once again among those present was Mrs Josephine Butler. She told the assembled audience that she was fighting for three aims:

- That by these Acts, the reputation, freedom and persons of women are placed absolutely in the power of the police.
- That it is unjust to apply the Acts to just one sex only and the punishments which they allow are degrading and brutalising.
- That a revolting vice is legalised by the Acts.

A petition was signed at the meeting by 128 local men and women from both the working and middle-classes but, despite this, the government refused to act until over 2 million signatures had been gathered nationwide, and the Acts were finally repealed in 1886. Even though it had taken almost eighteen years to achieve, Sheffield women had, by banding together, changed legislation but it was another group of women who were finally able to reach out to the girls caught up in prostitution in Sheffield against their will. These were wives of town councillors including Mrs D. Doncaster, Mrs H. J. Wilson and Mrs J. Wycliffe Wilson among others. Despite their high social standing they recognised that many of the girls had taken to the life through no fault of their own, and that one of the ways in which they were able to engage the girls was through Midnight Meetings. From that point on these were regularly held in Sheffield to which all were invited, and were so successful that it was noted that about fifty girls attended each evening. Tea was provided, as well as hymns and prayers and any of the women that were desirous of returning to the paths of virtue were invited to go to the House of Help. By using such methods women who had been forced to become prostitutes for reasons of economy, now found a way out of their terrible lives and back into respectable employment.

Prostitution continued to flourish in Sheffield, as it did in other towns and cities of Yorkshire. The difference now is that women have many more job opportunities through education than they had during this period of research. The impact of two world wars showed women that they could undertake employment which it was previously thought could only be done by men. Nevertheless, one battle they still had to overcome was a much more fundamental one.

CHAPTER FOUR

Maternity and Motherhood

During the late nineteenth and early twentieth century giving birth was very problematic for both mother and child. There were many dangers to newly-born infants including impure air, bad nursing, exposure to cold and improper food. At the same time the pregnant women themselves were susceptible to the unsanitary conditions in which a lot of the poorer classes lived, and puerperal fever was little understood; but the biggest danger facing mothers who gave birth in Sheffield was the risk of being attended by untrained midwives. Throughout the Victorian period the only qualification a midwife needed was usually to be a married woman who had several children of her own. It was estimated that in the town in October 1863 there was an average of 5,000–6,000 births a year, but experienced and qualified doctors from the Sheffield Dispensary were reluctant to attend to poorer patients as they often couldn't pay. So naturally those poor women had to make their own arrangements. The increasing number of deaths of women treated by untrained midwives gave concern at the time, but when a suggestion was made for the building of a specialist lying-in hospital to be built in the town, there was much opposition. The Sheffield Medical Officer, Dr Law pointed out that there was a lying-in ward at the Sheffield workhouse which was quite adequate for those unable to pay for the attentions of a professional surgeon. The workhouse at Fir Vale had, since its inception, trained nurses and midwives, but they were only available to pregnant women residing inside the workhouse itself.

Plaque indicating the site of Sheffield Hospital for Women.

When the deaths of pregnant women continued it was finally agreed that a new hospital called the Sheffield Lying-In Hospital would be established in January 1864. Local newspapers announced that a building had been acquired in Fig Tree Lane for the purpose and a matron had been appointed. Before it opened on 29 June 1864 it had been decided to name it the Sheffield Hospital for Women. It was intended that the hospital would have a staff of trained midwives, who would not only attend to the women on the wards, but would also visit poor women in their own homes. It was hoped that this would save them from the suffering they had received at the hands of ignorant and incompetent persons. Its remit was to train 'respectable women from the country to rid Sheffield of its ignorant and untrained midwives'. The Mayor, Mr Thomas Jessop was appointed president and a ladies committee was appointed; but it quickly became obvious that a major drawback was the fact that the hospital only had six beds. The following year another three beds were provided, but even these proved to be inadequate. At a guardian meeting at the Sheffield workhouse in January of 1864 it was noted that a previous lying-in hospital had been established in Sheffield twenty years earlier which had taken all cases of childbirth, but when puerperal fever broke out in the wards, it spread from bed to bed and because of that the hospital soon had to be closed.

Despite the opening of the new hospital, many poor women continued to use the services of untrained midwives, particularly those giving birth to illegitimate children. Miss Ellen Athorne, from Attercliffe, Sheffield was only 21 years of age when she died from injuries in her confinement, attended only by an untrained midwife, Elizabeth Charlton on 15 December 1864. At the inquest the jury was told that the poor woman had been in labour from 8 a.m. on the morning of 29 November 1864 to 8 p.m. that night. After such a prolonged labour and the severity of her pains, it was not surprising that the child was born dead. Witnesses said that the woman had begged for a surgeon to be called in, but Charlton had told her that there was no need for a professional man to attend and that 'nature would take its course'. The same witnesses reported that Charlton had used much violence in the delivery of the child and consequently Miss Athorne died just over two weeks later. A post mortem was held by surgeon Mr Herbert J. Walker who found parts of the victim's bladder and womb dreadfully torn, from which mortification had set in resulting in the woman's death. He told the jury that he had no hesitation in attributing her decease to malpractice on the part of the midwife. Mr Walker's assistant, Dr Davidson had attended Miss Athorne from after the confinement to her death, and he found the midwife Charlton to be ignorant of the proper care of the patient, and he too swore that he had never seen such terrible injuries before. On hearing this evidence Mrs Charlton swore she would never attend another confinement in this world. The coroner in his summing up spoke about the seriousness of the case when he said that the midwife:

had not shown competent skills and knowledge. The case was a very serious one, not only as regards the deceased woman and her offspring, but as regards society. For if midwives, totally ignorant of their duties, were allowed to act in this way, we must expect to have many more such deaths.

The jury found Elizabeth Charlton guilty of manslaughter and sent her for trial, which took place on 31 March 1865. The midwife was lucky in that her defence maintained that she had only taken the same steps that would have been taken by any experienced and skilful practitioner. After just half an hour's consultation the jury brought in a verdict of not guilty and she was discharged. Only ten years later the Sheffield Hospital for Women in Fig Tree Lane was found to be insufficient to serve its purpose and Thomas Jessop, a large steelworks manufacturer, offered to pay for the cost of another hospital to be built. He had been a prominent figure in Victorian Sheffield in 1863 when he was elected Master Cutler and then Lord Mayor. On 22 July 1878 the Jessop Hospital for Women was opened on Leavygreave Road costing nearly £30,000.

It was not only in Sheffield that pregnant women were dying. The problem was a national one and in an attempt to ensure that all pregnant women, regardless of status, were treated by a qualified midwife the government established the 1902 Midwives Act. The theory was that this would ensure that all midwives now had to have a qualification, and those found without one would be fined. A board was established and its remit was to regulate the issue of certificates for practising midwives and to provide training. However, these rules were hard to enforce as without any money, poorer women still chose local, unqualified women to care for them during confinement. The midwives themselves were very much against the Act as they saw it as depriving them not only of their employment, but also of their long-held status in society.

Eight years later in Sheffield the problems continued when another woman died after being treated by an unregistered midwife. But as the inquest showed, even a fully qualified medical practitioner's methods of treatment were found to be totally inadequate. The victim was a married woman of Carbrook Street, Sheffield called Alice Hartley. The inquest was held on 2 June 1910 and the jury were told that the deceased had been married to a carter, and that she had given birth to a daughter on 7 May assisted only by 72-year-old midwife, Charlotte Ransom of Corby Street, Sheffield. Although she was unregistered, Mrs Ransom had been allowed to continue to practise due to her twenty-six years' experience as a midwife. Six days after the birth on 13 May, Hartley had complained of feeling unwell and two days later Dr T.T. Somerville of Darnall, Sheffield was called in, where he diagnosed his patient to be suffering from pneumonia. On 18 May, as there was no improvement, he ordered her to be removed to the Firvale Workhouse Infirmary where she died on 30 May. Dr Godfrey Carter, the police surgeon held the post mortem and he found that the patient had died from pyaemia, which was an acute form of blood poisoning caused by the lack of proper treatment immediately after the birth of the child. Mrs Ransom was very indignant at his accusations, and stated that this was the first time in the whole of her career that she had ever had to attend a coroners' court. She told the jury that when Mrs Hartley had a relapse and became ill, she put it down to indigestion because of a new cake that the women had just eaten. The midwife claimed that she had always been very careful in her dealings with mothers and children and regularly used disinfectants.

Dr Somerville said that when he was first called in he made an external examination of the patient, and came to the conclusion that she was suffering from pneumonia. Mrs Ransom had assured him that she had taken every precaution at the birth, and consequently he did not think it necessary to look for any signs of blood poisoning. The police surgeon, Dr Carter interrupted the witness at this point, and told the jury that any woman feeling ill four or five days after a confinement must have shown some outward evidence that she was suffering from blood poisoning, which would have been obvious to any competent surgeon attending her. The coroner was shocked when a juror asked Dr Somerville whether he had taken the deceased woman's temperature and he admitted that he hadn't, as he had recently smashed his thermometer. The doctor was castigated by the coroner who told him that he should have made a more thorough examination of the deceased woman. The jury retired to consider their verdict and found that the midwife should be censured due to her inattention, but thought that she was not wilfully negligent. However, they were forced to lay the blame on Dr Somerville for not having made a much more thorough examination of the deceased than he had. The coroner also told Mrs Ransom that it would be a very serious thing for her if she ever figured in another case of this sort. In response the midwife muttered something about 'some people in this room who wished me harm and would like to take away the chance of earning my daily bread'.

On that occasion the midwife was let off with a caution, but the following month there was the first legal prosecution of an unqualified midwife in Sheffield, a woman called Ellen Webster of Eyre Lane. On 7 July 1910 the prosecution counsel, Mr Lang Coath explained to the magistrates at the City Police Court that not only was the woman uncertified, but she was also found to be unsatisfactory regarding her general cleanliness and efficiency. He added that although it was the first prosecution of a midwife in the city he hoped that it would not be the last. One of the female sanitary inspectors, Mrs Gertrude Frank told the court that she had examined the woman on 1 April 1910 and had warned her about practising without a certificate. She also gave evidence about the numbers of other women that the prisoner had attended since that warning. Mrs Webster offered no defence, apart from accusing the authorities of endeavouring to take away her livelihood. The chair to the magistrates, Mr B. Gledhill stated that in view of the fact that this was the first prosecution of a midwife in Sheffield, the court intended to be lenient with her. She was warned against practising without a certificate in the future, and bound over in the sum of £10 for twelve months.

It was not only the ignorance of the midwives that got blamed for the high mortality rates in Sheffield. When the Medical Officer of Health, Dr Robertson delivered his report to the Sheffield Health Committee in May 1899 he stated that more than a fifth of all deaths in Sheffield the previous year were those of infants under one year of age. He blamed these shocking statistics on the ignorance and apathy of the local mothers themselves. He asked for the appointment of women sanitary inspectors to improve the housing and health of the poor. Male sanitary inspectors had been employed for some time to keep the streets of the city repaired and free from filth. An experienced inspector was appointed at 30s a week and he was to be in charge of two inexperienced women to act as his assistants, to be appointed at 20s a week. Initially their remit was to visit and inspect workshops where women were employed, which was thought more suitable than the role being undertaken by a man. But gradually their remit changed following Dr Robertson's condemnation of the ignorance of mothers. It was decided that they would visit women in their homes, offering guidance and support throughout pregnancy in order to raise healthy children. These women were Mrs Florence Greenwood and Miss Edith Maynard, who were now to be responsible:

- To visit from house to house in the poorer districts of the city, and ascertain as to the general condition of rooms and bedrooms.
- To lend where necessary brushes for lime-washing.
- To give instruction as to the ventilation and cleansing of rooms and bedrooms.
- To see that bedclothes and clothing are kept reasonably clean.
- To see that children are properly fed, and where necessary to leave instructions as to feeding.

Just in that first year alone the two women visited 943 houses in the city where they recommended cleansing, white-washing and better ventilation. The attitude of the Medical Officer, Dr Robertson was very much the attitude of the medical authorities of the time. It was easier for the medical officials to simply put the number of deaths of mothers and infants down to the mothers' own ignorance, instead of addressing the fact that it was caused by the unsanitary conditions of the majority of the housing of the poor in Sheffield.

In a report on 'The Homes of the Poor in Sheffield' given by Miss Maynard on 13 February 1900 to the Christian Social Union, she described the lives of some of the women of Sheffield and the conditions in which they were living. She started by saying that for the last six months she had made around 4,000 visits to the homes of the poor in the city. Miss Maynard said that the courts in which the poor women of Sheffield lived were the worst she had ever seen. These courts were not paved and where the midden system still existed, many of these leaked and the stench was disgusting. The slop water ran out of sinks and remained standing in pools outside and one woman complained that she could not open her window for the smell emanating from the middens. Miss Maynard stated that it was very difficult to teach people the need to ventilate rooms, when the windows either could not open, or they were not able to open them because of the smell. Rats were in such abundance that the women and the children were afraid of them. Miss Maynard blamed the landlords for not carrying out repair works and had seen for herself people living in houses with leaky roofs and doors hanging off, which should by rights have been condemned. In several courts there was one tap which was the only water supply, but many were either leaking continually or running full bore and unable to be turned off. Lots of these houses had only one room downstairs and one room upstairs, in which all activities such as eating, sleeping and cooking had to be done. As an example she told the audience that in one bedroom, there were no bedsteads, but only mattresses on the floor. That room was shared by a man and wife, their son aged 21, a daughter aged 17, another son of 14 years and a girl of 10. Many of these people were not men down on their luck, but respectable church-going poor. In most cases if they complained to the landlord nothing was done or they were afraid to make a complaint in case they found themselves

Old unsanitary cottages at Darnall.

homeless. Miss Maynard concluded that what she was describing were not rare cases, but ordinary ones which she visited day in and day out, and urged that landlords visit the houses they rent and see for themselves the conditions in which their tenants lived. She ended, 'with those dilapidations inside and out, the homes of the poor in Sheffield were far from being the ideal cottage homes of England, which they might be supposed to be'.

Housing conditions in Sheffield would not be addressed until much later in the 1930s when a programme of slum clearance started to be implemented in the city. What these sanitary inspectors did was to give the women the tools they needed to make their own homes as sanitary as they possibly could under the circumstances. These women offered genuine and sensible advice as they encouraged new mothers to be aware of infant care, hygiene and the importance of giving their children nutritious meals. They also offered appropriate practical advice by encouraging new mothers to make cots out of banana boxes, rather than have a child sleeping in the same bed as adults or bigger siblings. By 1913 all newly appointed female sanitary inspectors also had to have a midwifery qualification, and those who didn't and were already in post were sent for training at the council's expense. At that time Sheffield had seventeen qualified female staff trained in midwifery, sanitation and nursing and gradually the days of the unqualified midwives came to an end. The Sheffield women sanitary inspectors were the trailblazers for the health visitors of the future. Interestingly enough this was one of the early roles for women which held no marriage bar. Most employers expected a woman to resign once her marriage was announced, but instead the role attracted many, both married or unmarried. As part of their job they were encouraged to study, attend lectures and improve themselves in a worthwhile and fulfilling role.

Little research has gone into the practice of birth control in the later years of the nineteenth century, and it was presumed by many married couples that the responsibility was always left up to the husband. As a consequence year after year women found themselves pregnant, having resigned themselves to the fact that there would be yet another mouth to feed. Many desperate women sent away for 'female pills' and various other concoctions to try to deal with the problem. Certainly there were plenty of quack remedies on the market, such as Mme Pellisair's Famous French Female Pills and Widow Welch's Pills for 'Irregularities in the Female System' which were freely advertised in the local newspapers of the period. However, they rarely helped, and many often caused more problems. It was not only married women that found themselves pregnant, and blame was placed on the many single women who were employed in the workshops and factories of the city. It was believed by the local authorities that working every day gave these women more freedom away from the scrutiny of their parents. Promiscuity was not by any means a recent problem. As early as 1837 a Sheffield doctor, George Holland had noted that women employed in the buffing of metal articles had a reputation for being 'fast'. He claimed that:

> the irresistible temptation which it offers to young females to discard the smooth and even tenor of

> domestic duties for the licentious freedom of the shop
> and its higher remuneration. The consequences flowing
> from this change; immorality, early marriages and their
> attendant evils, children and ignorant mothers.

Such promiscuous behaviour resulted in the birth of many
illegitimate children in Sheffield, and in the 1930s the city had
gained a dubious reputation for being notorious for the amount
of abortions which took place. On 24 May 1935 the *Sheffield
Independent* reported a statement made by Councillor W. Asbury
at the Sheffield Council of Women's Health Conference.
Speaking on the subject of maternal deaths due to abortion he
stated: 'Even if it should result in Sheffield being regarded as
an abortionists' city, we intend to focus public attention on this
grave problem, and shall continue to do so until this foul thing
disappears from our midst.'

The problem had started decades earlier when large numbers
of spontaneous abortions in Sheffield occurred in 1886 due to
lead poisoning being found in the town. It was finally traced
to the use of lead piping which took water from Redmires
reservoir into the town's water supply, and almost immediately
the problem was rectified. Nevertheless the deadly lesson had
been learned. For many years a lead plaster containing a plant
called diachylon had been used legally as a medicine. One
such treatment was ordered by a medical officer of health in
March 1856 for a consumptive workhouse patient for a plaster
containing diachylon to be placed on his chest. Not surprisingly
the man died, and there was little concern when, at his inquest
the medical officer revealed his treatment to the coroner. In
March 1861 a quack who had no medical qualifications, but
was called 'Dr. Kaye' by his patients, also prescribed a diachylon
plaster to be put onto the open wounds of a child aged 3. The
child had suffered severe burns from his nightshirt catching
fire. Naturally he too died and the quack was criticised for
treating the child without any medical experience. He stated in
his defence that he had applied such plasters before and found
them to do good.

At some point the distinction had been made and before long diachylon was made into pills and taken orally to induce an abortion, and horrifyingly many of these were sold by midwives. So it was with a certain amount of disgust that two certified Sheffield midwives were brought before the Sheffield Quarter Sessions on 24 October 1906 charged with supplying noxious pills containing diachylon. Mr Fleming for the prosecution, stated that it was hoped that the case would check the habit of supplying this drug which he claimed 'was all too prevalent in Sheffield at that time'. A midwife, Sarah Elizabeth Carford, aged 50, was charged with supplying the pills which had been handed over to one of the lady sanitary inspectors. Dr Godfrey Carter gave evidence and stated that 'I have been at so many bedsides when women have been made very ill by taking these pills' adding that diachylon should never be used for internal purposes. Mrs Carford said she had been a midwife for twenty years and lived on Infirmary Road, Sheffield and had twenty-one children of her own. She claimed to have bought her supply of the pills from a man who sold buttons and tapes from door-to-door. He had told her that they were quite safe as he got the recipe from a doctor. Carford was sentenced to twelve months imprisonment with hard labour. Another woman, Polly West aged 45 of Burnt Tree Lane, Sheffield, was also charged with supplying the same pills for a 'certain purpose'. She told the women to whom she supplied the pills 'keep it quiet as they are not registered by the government and I am not allowed to sell them'. Mrs West did not have any midwifery qualifications, and the recorder, Mr J. Scott-Fox took this into account when she was sentenced to six months imprisonment with hard labour.

Another case tried at the same sessions was that of a 25-year-old unnamed woman who regularly bought diachylon from a chemist on Westbar, Sheffield. The chemist gave evidence to say that he had sold her as much as a pound and a half of diachylon within three or four weeks. But in April 1906 he had refused to continue to supply her with the compound, as she had told him that she made them into pills. The defendant told the court that her uncle and aunt had been making the pills for over twenty-four years from their own recipe. When the pair had died she had taken the business over and sold them under the name of Nurse Oakley's Female Corrective Pills. However, she claimed that she did not sell them specifically as an abortifacient. The jury believed her story and returned a verdict of not guilty. At this time the increase in the number of abortions in Sheffield became so notorious that the subject was raised in the House of Commons by the MP for Ecclesall, Mr Samuel Roberts on 30 October 1906. He drew the Home Secretary's attention to the cases which had lately been tried in the Sheffield Court. Roberts suggested that the illegal preparation should in future be clearly labelled as a poison. Mr Gladstone told him that he had heard of the cases in Sheffield, but to have diachylon scheduled as a poison would entail a great deal of inconvenience, without having the desired object. He said that he hoped that the convictions at Sheffield would act as a sufficient deterrent, but the cases of abortion continued.

Courtroom at Leeds Assizes where Luke Reuben Watts was tried in March 1826.

It was not just the pills that were used, but there were people in the town who were prepared to perform abortions on women not wishing to increase their families any more. The police had great difficulty in gaining evidence in such cases, due to the very secretive nature of the offence. On 29 March 1876 a man practising as a medical botanist, Luke Reuben Watts of Pond Street, Sheffield was tried at the Leeds Assizes, charged with feloniously attempting to procure an abortion on 11 August the previous year. He was described as an old man of 67 years, but it was said that he had long been known as a practitioner in 'nefarious arts' and had been visited by many local women who found themselves in 'peculiar difficulties'. Watts claimed that he did not ask too many questions for the services he provided, for which he charged a hefty fee, although the operation was not always successful, and it was following one such case that he was caught. He had performed the operation on a woman called Sherwin, who became so ill that she thought that she was dying and was forced to call in a professional doctor. When the details came out, Watts was sent to take his trial at the assizes, but once there legal technicalities resulted in the man walking away Scot free. Two other women were due to give evidence against Watts, but because they had also received his criminal attentions, they were judged to be equally complicit in the crime. The judge discussed the case at length with his colleagues, but as it was well known in law that the evidence of an accomplice must be corroborated, and simply because there was no other evidence, the jury had no option but to dismiss the case. Another Sheffield man was not so lucky. Henry Simmonite was also tried at the assizes in May 1887 for the same offence. Once again the police had great difficulty in getting any evidence against him, as the local women concerned were only too anxious to avoid exposure of themselves. Twenty-five years earlier he had attracted the attention of the police by his alleged 'fortune telling'. Since that time he had been under constant police scrutiny and they witnessed his rooms being visited by young and old, married and unmarried females. Many women had been questioned about their visits, but nothing was proved against him until he left a woman called Drew in a dying condition. Knowing that her death was near and she had nothing left to lose, she was finally able to give the police the information they needed. Simmonite was arrested and tried with his two female accomplices. He was given penal servitude for life.

As we have seen, the fault of the high death rate of children was placed firmly on the mothers and in 1907 the Sheffield Motherhood League was formed. At the inaugural meeting at the Town Hall held on 29 May the Lady Mayoress, Mrs Robert Styring presided. The aim of the league was threefold and they were quite simply:

- To create higher ideals of parentage and home life
- To lessen infantile mortality
- To promote the welfare of children.

Regular lectures were given by lady doctors and they encouraged mothers to breast feed and to correctly care for their babies. By November 1911 the League had over 2,000 members and it was rapidly growing throughout the city. Alongside this the Sheffield health authorities were beginning to take an interest, not only in maternal needs, but also in the children's welfare. Many working mothers were forced to give their babies cows' milk, but it was noted in a Sheffield Council Meeting in April 1916 by Councillor Samuel Roberts that this was adding to the infant mortality rates. He gave startling figures showing that the skimming and adulteration of milk was seriously on the increase in Sheffield, and called attention to the fact that infants and young children were the worse affected by it. The Lord Mayor, Councillor F.A. Warlow agreed, and stated that it was their duty to stamp out the crime of milk adulteration in the city. Almost immediately a series of prosecutions took place and in one such case, milk vendor Herbert B. Mortimer admitted selling milk which contained 9.5 per cent water and he was fined £5. However, the police found it very difficult to bring such prosecutions to court, as they discovered the devious way in which milk sellers operated. Many vendors had two containers side by side, one containing unadulterated milk and the other just water, which would be added for unwary customers. When officials approached to test the milk, the unadulterated milk was freely given, thereby evading prosecutions. In order to combat this Maternity and Child Welfare clinics were set up by the health authorities which sold powdered milk for babies.

MARRIED LOVE

A New Contribution to the Solution of Sex Difficulties

By MARIE STOPES, D.Sc., Ph.D.

"Clear, thoughtful, penetrating. . . . Our advice is for women to read it, and for men to read it."—*English Review*.

"An extremely sensible little book. . . . Really needed as a public adviser."—*Lancet*.

AT ALL BOOKSELLERS, 6/- NET

G. P. PUTNAM'S SONS, LTD.

24 BEDFORD ST., STRAND, LONDON, W.C.2

Advert for Marie Stopes' book on birth control.

By July 1923 a Child Welfare Centre had been opened in Norfolk Street which had been visited by 800–900 mothers each week. There they could have the baby weighed and seek any advice from the doctors and nurses in attendance, as well as buying the tins of powdered milk in place of tinned milk their mothers had used. On Saturdays the clinic was devoted to the needs of pregnant mothers, who were seen by doctors and advice was offered by nurses. It was not known how many of these women asked for advice on birth control, but in April 1920 a book advocating the limiting of families written by Marie Stopes was advertised in the *Sheffield Independent* at 6s each. The question of birth control was a very controversial one and it attracted much public attention in the city. At the time many leading authorities truly believed that it would lead to greater promiscuity in women, which would increase the numbers of sexually transmitted diseases. Others praised it and advocated for it to be introduced in all the Maternity and Child Welfare clinics across the city. Certainly it was noted by August 1923 that there had been a great reduction of infant mortality rates in Sheffield. The Medical Officer, Dr Frederick E. Wynne stated that twenty years previously, the figures had been 200 children per 1,000 of the population and two years previously had fallen to 80 per 1,000 population. He was an advocate of birth control and it was announced in October of the same year that he would give a lecture on birth control at the Victoria Hall, Sheffield on 11 October. A large audience attended as he spoke about the benefits of contraception, but there was much opposition from the Roman Catholic Church. Nevertheless by May 1933 books on birth control were readily advertised in the local press such as *Aids to Family Limitation* and *Birth Control: Its Use and Abuse*. The controversy continued, and it was not until the Sheffield Women's Welfare Committee took control and opened a clinic at Attercliffe that family limitation advice was given, but only to married women.

The Sheffield Women's Welfare Clinic opened in May 1933 at Attercliffe Vestry Hall. The name had been selected due to the controversial attitude towards the subject of birth control, and it was decided that it would be called a 'welfare clinic'. The women who made up the committee and who ran the new clinic were headed by the Lady Mayoress of Sheffield. Indeed three of its first visitors were women who, rather than wanting birth control advice, instead wanted advice on getting pregnant and all three later succeeded. Another case was a woman who had thirteen pregnancies, but which had resulted in only one child being born alive. Women who asked for advice on birth control often had from six to fourteen children and wished to limit their families for economic reasons. The medical officer of the clinic Dr Margaret Owen, also gave marital advice to brides before marriage and on motherhood to new mothers. In February 1938 the committee were asking for funds to allow them to open another welfare clinic in some of the more distressed areas of the city. One Sheffield man who condemned the idea of birth control wrote to the editor of the *Sheffield Independent* suggesting that 'there is no real demand for this wretched business, otherwise public support would have been sufficient'.

THE BEST METHODS OF SCIENTIFIC BIRTH CONTROL

Will be taught to any married woman at the
SHEFFIELD WOMEN'S WELFARE CLINIC,
ATTERCLIFFE VESTRY HALL,

Every Tuesday, from 6.0 to 8.0 p.m., and in addition the first and third Tuesdays in the Month, 2.30 to 4.0 p.m.

Every patient will be seen in private by a qualified Woman Doctor.

CONSULTATION FEE—MINIMUM OF ONE SHILLING

(No charge for subsequent visits within the year).

Closed for Bank Holiday weeks, and the whole of August. This is a Voluntary Clinic. Please give as generously as you can.

Advert for advice on birth control at Women's Welfare Clinic.

The clinic also advertised that any married women could now have a private consultation at the Welfare Clinic, with a qualified female doctor, in ways of limiting her family. It was stated at the time that although opinion on the topic was frowned upon in some quarters, no such lecture would have been possible thirty years earlier. Dr Owen told a reporter in April 1945 that during the past year, 209 new patients had attended the clinic and many of these had been referred by doctors and nurses. The Sheffield Women's Welfare Clinic had their own link with the Family Planning Association by 1950, and were foremost in advocating that sex education be provided in schools.

The women of Sheffield had learned from many experiences that to have any effect they had to take responsibility in order to make changes. Thankfully those women of position, mainly councillors' wives led by the Lady Mayoress, recognised the need to educate ordinary women with the introduction of family limitation and aspiring to raise healthy children. Many of the women who later were elected onto Sheffield City Council made mothers and children their priority. The introduction of the women as sanitary inspectors did much towards helping mothers to help themselves, and to understand the need for hygiene and healthy feeding of their children. However, in order to gain equality with men, the struggle was to become very difficult and had much deeper roots.

CHAPTER FIVE

The Long March towards Equality Begins

Sheffield was notable in history for being one of the first towns to demand equality for women, long before the age of the suffragettes. The beginning of the struggle was mainly due to a social reformer, Anne Knight from Chelmsford. She had been invited along with Mary Anne Rawson of Wincobank Hall, Sheffield to a conference on slavery in London in 1840. Both women were appalled at the fact that, although many women attended, none of them were allowed to speak. Anne Knight also corresponded with a Mrs Rooke of Sheffield, whose name she had been given by an outspoken Sheffield Chartist leader, Isaac Ironside. Anne Knight and Mary Anne Rawson urged the women of Sheffield to band together and demand equality with men. Together with Anne Kent they were invited to form the Sheffield Women's Political Association. The inaugural meeting was held at the Democratic Temperance Hotel, at 33 Queen Street, Sheffield on 5 February 1851. Significantly a woman, Mrs Abiah Higginbottom, was appointed to take the chair. Another local woman, Mrs C. Ash was appointed as temporary president, and she laid down the very first manifesto for female suffrage. Mrs Ash began by referring to the many plans, systems and organisations which had been laid down by men for the better government of the people. According to the *Northern Star & Leeds General Advertiser* she addressed her audience as 'sisters' and demanded that women be included in gaining the vote,

MEETING AT SHEFFIELD.—THE RIGHTS OF WOMEN.

A public meeting of females was held on Wednesday evening, February 5th, in the Democratic Temperance Hotel, 33, Queen-street, for the purpose of reading the Queen's speech, and also to adopt a petition to parliament for the enfranchisement of adult females. Mrs. Obiate Higginbottom was called upon to preside. After she had read the speech, the following motion and petition were unanimously agreed to :—" That, seeing the Queen is enjoying her prerogative as a woman, this meeting is of opinion that until the entire enfranchisement of women is conceded, justice will not be done ; therefore, this meeting resolve to petition the legislature for the enactment of a bill which will enfranchise the whole female adult population of this empire, and that the following be the petition :—

" To the Honourable the Commons of Great Brittain and Ireland in Parliament assembled,

" The humble petition of the female inhabitants of Sheffield, in the County of York, in public meeting assembled, held on Wednesday evening, in the Democratic Temperance Hotel, Queen-street, Feb. 5th, 1851,

" Sheweth, that we, the females of Sheffield do approach your honourable house with all due respect, to make known our desires and opinions upon a subject which we consider is a right withheld, but which, legitimately, belong to our sex, the enfranchisement of women. Therefore, we beseech your honourable house to take into your serious consideration the propriety of enacting an electoral law, which will include adult females within its provisions, and your petitioners will ever pray."

The next resolution was " That the foregoing petition be entrusted to Mr. John Parker, the borough member, for presentation, and that John Arthur Roebuck, his colleague, be requested to support the same."

Thanks beeing voted to the chair, the meeting broke up.

Report of first meeting of the SWPA.

> as we are the majority of the nation, and it is a birthright
> equally with our brothers to vote for the man who is to
> sway our political destiny. Are women to continue to be
> the drudges of society? We the women of the democracy
> of Sheffield answer No! We put forth the earnest appeal
> to our sisters of England to join hand and heart with
> us in this noble and just cause, to the exposing and
> eradicating such a state of things.

She urged all the women of England to 'shake off their apathy and to raise their voices for right and liberty until justice be conceded'. In conclusion Mrs Ash called on them 'to aid us in completing this holy work of liberty and fraternity'. The meeting ended with a proposal that a petition to be sent to local MP, Mr James Parker to present to both Houses of Parliament from the women of Sheffield. In the House of Lords the chosen champions to present the petition were George Howard the Earl of Carlisle and Lord Brougham. Although there was little response from the government, the Sheffield Women's Political Association received much eager support from women all over England and France. These were ordinary women who immediately recognised that any fundamental change would have to come with political intervention, which could not be achieved until women got the vote.

The local press also noted that the times were changing on 8 February 1851 when the *Sheffield Independent* predicted that:

> the men of Sheffield are little aware that a formidable
> movement was made by the female inhabitants of the
> borough of Sheffield in a public meeting, assembled
> last Wednesday night. We are informed that it was an
> enthusiastic meeting. It seems that selfish men had been
> agitating for the Charter to enfranchise themselves
> alone, and the result had been a signal failure. Now the
> women of Sheffield were about to take on that fight for
> themselves. Seeing that the Queen is in the enjoyment
> of her prerogative as a woman, the meeting was of the
> opinion that until the enfranchisement of women is

> conceded, justice will not be done; therefore the meeting
> resolved to petition both Houses of Parliament for the
> enactment of a bill which will enfranchise the whole
> female adult population of this empire.

Even though the reporter was obviously impressed at the
importance of such an historical event, by the time of the
next meeting it was run on more conventionally genteel lines.
Therefore the next meeting was introduced as a 'Soiree and a
Ball' which was held at the Hall of Science on 22 April 1851,
nevertheless the two main speakers were women. Mrs Ash
delivered a speech on the 'Enfranchisement of Women' followed
by Mrs Higginbottom who delivered a lecture on 'The Industry
and Independence of Women'. To conclude the meeting
Mrs Higginbottom proposed to send a memorial to Lord John
Russell, a leading Whig and Liberal politician in favour of the
principles of universal suffrage, which was agreed with much
enthusiasm. Despite this rousing decision, it was reported that
by 9 p.m. the speeches were brought to a close, before Mr Isaac
Ironside 'led off with one of the ladies of the committee to
commence the dancing, which continued up to midnight'.

On the evening of 25 November 1851 Anne Knight returned
to Sheffield to speak on the 'Rights of Women' at another
meeting described once more as a 'soiree' held at the Council
Hall, Sheffield. Of the sixty persons present in the audience, it
was estimated that almost two thirds were made up of females.
Once again, the proceedings were quiet and dignified and began
with some Hungarian refugees singing some of their national
airs, 'whilst some of the party availed themselves of their cigars,
and others promenaded about'. Miss Knight was described as
being 'a lady of middle age, of very bland and prepossessing
countenance with a cultured and refined mind' as the principal
speaker. She spoke about her regular visits to France, where the
women there were so passionate about women's rights, that two
of them had been imprisoned. Miss Knight was followed by
Mrs Higginbottom who delivered a 'Declamation against Man's
Tyranny' and 'Women's Wrongs' which was heavily criticised

RIGHTS OF WOMEN.—On TUESDAY Evening, a SOIREE will be held in the Council Hall, at Six o'Clock. After Tea, Miss ANNE KNIGHT, of Chelmsford, hopes to Address the Meeting at Half-past Seven. Admission, 1s. each. A Memorial to Lord J. Russell, in favour of the principles of Universal Suffrage, will be proposed for adoption

Advert for Rights of Women Soiree.

by a local reporter. He stated that 'one might have thought from the monotonous strain of complaint and demands, that the female sex in this country were little better than slaves'. He concluded that:

> In no country, in no age in the world has woman been so honoured, or exercised so great an influence over society as in England at this moment. We would advise our peripatetic female lecturers to go to some far off land, unblessed by the humanizing influence of Christianity, where they may find a more needy sphere of labour and where the state of society will not present so palpable a demonstration of the absurdity of their agitation.

It is perhaps this kind of criticism that influenced the way in which the Women's Association was to run, as at the first annual conference held on 25 February 1852 in the Committee Rooms on Queen Street, there was a totally different agenda. Instead of concentrating on the enfranchisement of their sex, the Association's concerns were targeted against the enrolment of the militia and in condemning war. Although some further lectures were delivered in April on the subject of 'Rights of Women' they also included 'Dress Reform', and the 'Inequality of the Marriage Law' before the Sheffield Women's Rights Association finally sunk into merciful oblivion. The *Reynolds's Newspaper* dated 21 December 1853 accounts for its early demise, and concluded 'the recent meetings in Sheffield were before their time'. Discussions on universal suffrage were everywhere and it was even deliberated at the Sheffield town council meeting on 8 October 1851. Possibly remembering the enthusiasm at the first meeting of the Women's Association, Alderman Dunn asked the council what they would do 'as to the women', to which there was no response just loud laughter in the chamber. Although he added that in his opinion 'women would vote better than many men did' the subject was quickly changed. Another Alderman, Mr Hadfield, simply expressed the prevalent view of the period concluding that 'wives should manage the inside of the house and their husbands any outside affairs.'

The subject of equal rights for women continued to be discussed and ridiculed in the town and the local newspaper even took up the cause on 20 April 1868. The *Sheffield and Rotherham Independent* commented that, 'Anxiety on such a subject is not unlikely to unsettle the minds of spinsters as they verge towards thirty, and may lead them into many rashnesses besides that of joining the National Society for Women's Suffrage.'

Many local people felt the same, as indicated by a letter condemning women's suffrage believing that women were incapable of understanding politics. The letter signed simply MATERFAMILIAS was printed in the *Sheffield Independent* dated 22 September 1868 and stated:

> Of all the absurd bills that have been introduced into Parliament, the Women's Suffrage Bill, was I think, the most absurd. I certainly cannot see the slightest right that women have to interfere in the government of a country; she was never created to make laws wherewith to govern a man.

Quoting the old chestnut from the Bible that 'thy desire shall be unto thy husband and he shall rule over thee' the letter writer claimed that 'not one woman in 500 would take the trouble to study politics'. Apologising for troubling the editor at all, the writer concluded that

A WOMAN'S OPINION OF FEMALE SUFFRAGE.

To THE EDITOR.—It gave me much pleasure to read the decision Mr. C. T. Forster came to with regard to the enfranchisement of women. Of all the absurd bills that have been introduced into Parliament, the Women's Suffrage Bill was, I think, the most absurd. I certainly cannot see the slightest right that women have to interfere in the government of a country; she was never created to make laws wherewith to govern man. When Adam and Eve were expelled from Paradise, we are distinctly told that God said unto the woman, "Thy desire shall be unto thy husband, and he shall rule over thee." I imagine the ladies of the Miss Becker school would say it is quite useless to argue in this way, we have no husbands to rule over us, therefore our desire is not unto our husbands, but unto the government of the nation. Now, I believe there is not one woman in five hundred that would take the trouble to study politics. Give women the suffrage and you give them more power than the Queen of England exercises, for she takes no part in the political government of the country without consulting her ministers. In my humble opinion, if women ever obtain the franchise it will have a degrading effect upon their minds; for, once they begin to mix freely with the opposite sex, they will lose that native delicacy which now gives them their legitimate influence in society. Miss Becker informs us that she hopes the time will come when women will cease to use the needle. If that time ever come, alas for the babies! Are they to be sent forth in a toilet similar to that in which the youthful Britons gloried!

Apologising for troubling you, I have the honour to be, yours sincerely,   MATERFAMILIAS.
September 19th, 1868.

Letter from MATERFAMLIAS condemning Votes for Women.

> if women ever obtain the franchise it will have a
> degrading effect upon their minds; for once they begin
> to mix freely with the opposite sex, they will lose that
> native delicacy which now gives them their legitimate
> influence in society.

The letter writer was simply articulating the thoughts of the period, but the following year on 28 September 1868 one of the few women prominent in the suffrage movement, who considered herself as representing the working-class, came to Sheffield to speak to local women. Miss Jessie Craigen, an avid speaker on behalf of women's rights, warned the audience collected in the Temperance Hall that any woman attempting to advocate for equal rights would be subject to much ridicule. She said that men had made and passed laws which were most unjust for women, before debarring those same women from protesting with any effect against the hardships laid upon them. Miss Craigen gave as an example the many cases of seduction and breach of promise which had been tried at the assizes and reminded the audience how women had little legal presence in law.

There was so much agitation that eventually, no doubt as a sop to women suffragists, Parliament passed the Municipal Franchise Act which was brought into force on 1 November 1869. This would enable widows or single women ratepayers to vote in local elections, despite the fact that many believed that women would not use their vote rationally. However, the vote was not extended to married women as it was generally agreed that their husbands voted for them as the household franchise. The same day as the Act came into being there were elections in several wards of Sheffield, where it was noted with satisfaction that those women who were eligible had indeed used their votes. It was also noted on that occasion, that the elected councillors had received many more votes than they had in previous years. A few months later in May of 1870 it was predicted in the *Sheffield Independent* that the tide for local women was finally turning when it stated that:

> The ladies live in fine times when the Lords of Creation
> are pricked in conscience and feel that they have been
> doing the women a great injustice. They have admired
> the fair sex, have given them love, homage, a practical
> domestic supremacy, and shelter from many of the
> hardships and responsibilities of life. But they have had
> a sort of regard for the Scriptural maxim that the man is
> the head of the woman, and therefore have restrained, at
> least in name, the guidance of affairs. Now, however, they
> are penitent and have entered upon a course of reform.

No matter how penitent the 'Lords of Creation' might have felt, they had no intention of giving ordinary women the vote for many years to come.

Miss Jessie Craigen had recognised the need to appeal to 'ordinary' women in her campaign for women's rights, and so when she returned to Sheffield in the summer of 1879 instead of hiring halls and rooms, she went to places where the people of Sheffield worked. On 5 June it was arranged that she would hold a meeting simply on waste ground by the church at Heeley. It was reported that when Miss Craigen had gone to the house of the persons who had agreed to help her to arrange the meeting, she found them out. Undaunted, she erected a platform herself and using a hand bell to attract her audience, soon had a fine meeting of working men and women around her. She spoke about the need for women to be held as equal to men, to which there was much enthusiasm from the crowd. Her strategy of holding these open air meetings was very successful at reaching out to large numbers of working men and women of the town. A few days later on the afternoon of 14 June 1879, Miss Craigen held another open air meeting by the cricket field at Carbrook after the match had finished, and standing on a large egg chest surrounded by people, she began to speak. It was reported that also in the audience, eager to hear her, was a large party of very well-dressed women who stood close in order to hear every word. As had already been noted Jessie was a very impressive speaker and on 22 July after hearing her at the Temperance Hall, Duke Street, Park, a certain Mr Cook of Sheffield declared:

> I never thought about women's suffrage, except that it was a good joke, until Miss Craigen came, but I have been at plenty of her meetings since except one, and I saw plainly that there was no joke in it. It is awful serious. I think it is a working class question, for when women ask for justice, they ought to have it. I for one would do all I could to get it for them.

Following the example of Miss Craigen, the women of Sheffield were beginning to wake up to the inequality of their sex, and more and more demands for female suffrage were being made.

So there was much excitement in the town when it was announced that another large meeting was due to be held on 27 February 1882 which was to be chaired by Viscountess Harberton, who earlier that year had written a pamphlet on 'Observations on Women's Suffrage'. On the night of the meeting it was reported that the body of Sheffield's Albert Hall was crowded with local women, as were the galleries which surrounded it. On the platform with the viscountess were other female suffragists, not only from Sheffield but from London, Manchester and Leeds. Viscountess Harberton was greeted with great applause, as she addressed the audience, before condemning the law that refused the vote to women. She told them:

> Ladies, as I stand here tonight to bid you all welcome, and feel myself one of this vast assembly of women met together to protest against the continuance of a law which may well be said to be the foundation of all those laws we have so long petitioned against. It alone has made, and does make, them impossible. I cannot help feeling glad of one thing. I am glad to see that all of you, as evidenced by your presence here, are one with me in

the knowledge that it is in this lies our greatest danger, and until we can get it altered we are living on social quicksand.

Local speaker Mrs Charlotte Wilson (wife of Councillor Henry Joseph Wilson) admitted that due to the position of her husband, she would get no direct personal advantage from the granting of suffrage to Sheffield women. Nevertheless she put forward her own personal take on the suffrage question. Mrs Wilson stated that as the mother of growing-up sons she had her own role to play. She believed that one of her first duties was to make the home as pleasant and attractive as she possibly could. But that the knowledge gained by mothers and sisters would allow them to converse intelligently on political questions. By doing so it would not only increase the attractiveness of the home, but would 'exercise a most beneficial effect upon the political life of the whole nation'. Other female speakers from other towns spoke of how they looked forward with interest to seeing the progression of the movement in Sheffield. Once again the local newspaper dated 28 February 1882 was quick to realise the importance of the meeting as the reporter noted:

> A large and enthusiastic meeting was held last evening at the Albert Hall, Sheffield in favour of extending the suffrage to women. The hall was crowded, the body and the galleries being filled with women. Some of the seats in the galleries were occupied by gentlemen, but even there the ladies largely predominated.

The petition from the demonstration by the women of Sheffield was presented to the House of Commons by Mr Mundella the Liberal MP for Brightside, a month later on 17 March 1882.

No matter how enthusiastic the women of Sheffield might have felt, the government was slow to make any changes, although one significant change was the introduction of the Elementary Education Act which had taken place in 1870. This Act which initially was not seen as the first step in the gaining of the vote, slowly began to place women in a position of some authority. It had set the framework for the way in which all schools in Britain should be run, and laid out the compulsory education for boys and girls from the ages of 5–12 years. From this act the creation of local school boards was established in all towns and cities, which naturally consisted entirely of male members who were elected every three years. The irony, which was noted at the time, was that there were three female teachers employed to each male, who were paid much lower wages. Inevitably, then the question had to be asked as to why there were no women elected onto the Sheffield School Board. It had been asked at a Women's Suffrage Meeting held at Attercliffe on 27 February 1882, and it was a question which the school board could not ignore. As a result of this when the elections were scheduled to take place in November of that year, it was finally announced that a woman had put herself forward as a candidate for the election. She was Mrs Sarah Ruth Wilson, the wife of Mr J. Wycliffe Wilson, a councillor and glass and china dealer of Sheffield. On 22 November 1882 Mrs Wilson made history when she was elected onto the Sheffield School Board with 11,786 votes. In her speech she told the board that she was delighted to be elected, as she felt the education of girls was just as important as it was for boys. However, despite the board's initial enthusiasm Mrs Wilson remained the only woman on the school board for a further six years, before being joined by another local woman, Mrs Mary Ann Palmer Ripper.

The Local Government Act of 1894 finally gave all women, irrespective of marital status, the right to elect and to stand for election in parish councils, district councils, and as poor law guardians. On 4 December 1894 the Sheffield workhouse guardians received a nomination for Mrs Elizabeth Chappell of Spital Hill, Sheffield to be elected onto the board. Once again it was ground breaking as, although there were several other male applicants, she was the only woman nominated. Two days later she was successfully elected, yet for another thirteen years she was the only female workhouse guardian in the whole of the city. There is little information about how Mrs Chappell, Mrs Wilson or Mrs Ripper were received by the other male members of the school or workhouse board, or whether they had been made to feel welcome, but the evidence suggests that other Sheffield women were not exactly queuing up to join them. A letter to the editor printed in the *Sheffield Independent* of 2 February 1907 spoke about workhouse-guardian Mrs Chappell who had at that time been serving on the board for the past 12½ years. The writers of the letter, Dr Helen M. Wilson and Alice J. Watson finally suggested that it was time that other women be appointed in her place. They stated that 'we cannot believe that she is the only woman in this great city who is able and willing to undertake such work'. The letter suggested that women were eminently suited to the role of workhouse guardian and hoped that:

> some sensible woman might be appointed who could do much more towards the upbringing of the workhouse children, by using various economies she has already practised in her own home. By such methods she would be saving the pockets of the ratepayers as well as helping out in the female wards of the hospitals and infirmaries. The service of the poor has always been considered a fitting sphere for Christian women, and in these latter years ladies of the highest social position, as well as the wives of working men, have ungrudgingly given time and thought to this arduous and painful service, and have shown that thereby they need sacrifice no whit of their refinement or womanliness.

As well as the letter, a meeting was also held in the South Street Methodist schoolroom on the same subject on 19 March 1907. One of the principal speakers Dr Maud Cavanagh said that the first essential for any guardian was an intimate knowledge of the poor, their home lives and their needs. More than anything it should be someone who had previously worked among them as she had done. Dr Cavanagh claimed not to be a promoter who said that men and women were equal, as she felt that they were so vastly different both physically and mentally, but she believed that they were suited to support each other's work. Mr George Abbott stated that he too was a believer in the equality of the sexes, but he truly believed that a woman's place was in the home. However, he was not one of those who thought that a woman could do no work outside the home, and therefore he felt that any women should qualify as a guardian of the poor. The flood doors were opened, and later that month there were five other Sheffield women seeking election onto the board of guardians. The two successful women that were elected were Dr Maud Cavanagh and Mrs Annie Crowther who, it was said, were expected to introduce 'a healthy change in the administrative side of the workhouse'.

Meanwhile, inroads were being made in other areas. On 13 January 1900 a Miss J. Cleghorn of Heeley Bank School Board was installed as the very first female president of the Sheffield and District Teachers' Association. There had been women involved with the Association before, but they had only served in a minor capacity such as decorating rooms and providing refreshments. Despite this, Miss Cleghorn's election was undoubtedly a popular decision and she was loudly applauded from the audience composed entirely of men when she took her place. The new president then gave her address on the subject of 'Liberty, Equality and Fraternity' and its application to the teaching profession, but she was unable to resist a dig at the unfairness of the differences in salary between male and female teachers. Miss Cleghorn boldly stated that 'when women took the places of men in school, they should have been paid the same salary. Now as a result women teachers were preferred to men, simply because they were cheaper to employ.'

At the dawn of the twentieth century, more and more women were achieving positions which had seemed unattainable fifty years earlier. Slowly but surely Sheffield women were breaking down barriers and taking on roles of some responsibility, but it was the matter of female suffrage which took the longest to change. Despite the fact that the question had been bandied about in Sheffield since the formation of the Sheffield Women's

Political Association in 1851, it would take militant action and many more years for local women to achieve their ultimate goal. But little did the women of Sheffield know that over the next few years they would be involved in a national campaign which would shake up the lives of the people of the city. The gentle attempts to persuade the vote from a reluctant government would come to an end, as many Sheffield women would break loose from the chains which had bound them as second-class citizens. For a major part of the next few years, former respectable middle-class and working-class women of the city would take part in a militant struggle which would see them being sent to prison, breaking windows and bombing letter boxes in order to achieve that basic common right, equality with men.

CHAPTER SIX

The Sheffield Suffragettes

At the turn of the century the suffragists were becoming divided regarding the manner in which getting the vote should be achieved. Some believed in militant protest whilst others believed that it should be done by lobbying Parliament and using peaceful means. Mrs Pankhurst had thrown down the gauntlet by starting her own military campaign on 10 October 1903, when she formed the Women's Social and Political Union in Manchester. The WSPU adopted the slogan 'Deeds not Words' and encouraged women to do anything in their power to achieve their aims. So when the women of Sheffield heard that Rt. Hon. Mr Asquith MP was intending coming to the Norfolk Drill Hall, Sheffield, it was decided that something must be done. On the night of 4 January 1906 the Hall was so packed with over 6,000 Liberal supporters that there were only seats for half the audience, and the rest had to be content with standing room only. To begin with Mr Asquith, who the year before had been made Chancellor of the Exchequer, received resounding cheers from his fellow Liberals, but he had not been talking for long before an unnamed woman in the audience interrupted him. She stood up holding up a calico scroll with black lettering, on which was written 'VOTES FOR WOMEN'. The woman shouted out 'Will the new Government give women the vote?' Men in the audience that were near, tried to restrain her, but for eight minutes the woman stood on a chair and managed to resist all their efforts to quieten her. So insistent was she that police officers were finally called to remove her. As she was being taken from the hall, Mr Asquith told his audience:

> Ladies and Gentlemen I am exceedingly sorry that it is necessary to remove anybody from a meeting of this kind, more particularly any member of the other sex, but I cannot help thinking that no good cause is served, or effectively served, by disrupting a public meeting.

The Rt. Hon. Gentleman had no idea what was to come! Mr Asquith had barely began to speak again before, in what was obviously a concerted planned attack, another woman rose and began the same haranguing of the MP. When she too was removed, a further woman described only as 'Miss Pankhurst from Manchester, who has achieved notoriety by her persistence in drawing attention to the claims of women suffragists', also stood on a chair and waved her arms about, addressing the same question to Mr Asquith. When she too was removed, resisting violently, yet another woman was dealt with similarly. In total four women were ejected from the meeting at the Drill Hall. At that time the local newspapers did not know what to make of the sudden attack, as they observed that all four of the unnamed ladies who had subverted the meeting had all

Mrs. Whitworth.

Mrs Edith Whitworth, a well-known Sheffield activist for WSPU.

been visitors to the city, and that no local women were actually involved.

Doubt was cast on this statement shortly afterwards when Sheffield formed its own branch of the Women's Social and Political Union with Mrs Edith Whitworth as the secretary. She was a working-class woman who lived on Wath Road, Nether Edge, Sheffield, with her two small children and her husband, who was a postal worker. Mrs Whitworth was to become a well-known activist for the suffragette cause, and even at the time was described as being 'one of the WSPU's most enthusiastic disciples'. In September 1906 the Sheffield WSPU invited what was described as an advance guard of what were now being called 'suffragettes' to the city. They consisted of Miss Mary E. Gawthorpe, a teacher and socialist of Leeds and Miss Annie Kenney from Saddleworth. It is tempting to think that Miss Kenney had attended Mr Asquith's disrupted meeting months earlier, as it was known that she had been imprisoned for thirteen days for disturbing a meeting in exactly the same manner, by shouting out and holding up a banner. On 21 September 1906 Miss Gawthorpe began her campaign in Sheffield by a series of open air meetings in Town Hall Square, which was attended by large crowds listening attentively to what she was saying. Afterwards Miss Gawthorpe told a reporter that she intended, whilst she was in Sheffield, to talk to women in their own homes and try to interest them in joining the WSPU because 'if women wanted the vote, they would only achieve it by united action'. Miss Gawthorpe, taking a leaf out of Miss Craigen's book, also planned to hold open air lunchtime meetings at places where many Sheffield women were largely employed.

When it became known that Richard Haldane, the Secretary of State for War, was coming to Sheffield to give a speech at the Albert Hall on 20 November 1907, it was reported that the local authorities were nervously anxious to protect him from attacks by local suffragettes. The *Sheffield Daily Telegraph* reported that all women entering the hall would undergo a most searching examination. All the cellars, skylights and windows were carefully examined, and a man was employed to look under all the seats before the doors were opened. All this to prevent any demonstrations by what was now disparagingly labelled 'the shrieking sisterhood'. But suffragette action against Mr Haldane started before he had even arrived at the Sheffield railway station. One intrepid unnamed woman, forbidden to gain entrance to the railway station when the minister's train was due to arrive, decided instead to daub his car, which was parked outside, with the slogan 'Votes for Women'. When Mr Haldane exited the station therefore, he was forced to drive off in a car with the suffragettes motto daubed all over the vehicle. When he arrived for a visit at the University on Western Bank he was reminded by a group of women that twenty years previously he had drafted a bill to remove all the disabilities that the law puts upon women having the vote, and that they were still waiting for that same bill to be introduced.

Anticlimactically, the same newspaper reports were dismissive of the Sheffield women's actions at the hall that evening. It was gleefully reported that there were only eleven suffragettes to meet Mr Haldane, which included the Misses Adela Pankhurst, Kenney and Gawthorpe. They were described as 'grim, determined, excited, garrulous and angry women'. Not surprisingly they were refused permission to enter by the steward, who also castigated them for their unwomanly behaviour. To the women's frustration they were also restrained from entering the hall by the deputy chief constable of Sheffield, the chief inspector and several burly police officers. To their disgust they were forced to watch as several other women entered the hall accompanied by their 'highly respectable, Liberal male friends'. Their annoyance was complete, when news was given to Miss Adela Pankhurst and her 'lieutenant' Miss Kenney that Mr Haldane was already inside the hall, having come through a side entrance. Around 8 p.m. Miss Pankhurst and Miss Kenney made a sudden rush towards the doors leading into the saloon area, past the steward and a constable, who seized Miss Pankhurst around the waist. He was quickly assisted by more constables who managed to restrain her. Miss Kenney was also prevented from going through the doors and the two women were 'dragged, pushed and finally carried outside through the front doors of the Albert Hall'. Miss Pankhurst was undaunted as she took the opportunity, now hatless and from a position clinging onto a drain pipe, to address a huge crowd which stretched across Barkers Pool.

Not surprisingly the *Sheffield Independent* wrote:

> There were some demonstrations on the part of the suffragettes who have haunted the city during the last few weeks and who gained access to the vestibule of the Albert Hall. But beyond a great deal of noise and much bustle, there was nothing to note.

On 29 November it was decided that the Sheffield WSPU meetings would now be held monthly for all those 'interested in questions relating to women's position in national life'. Now Sheffield would be regularly visited by women who had led the cause for female suffrage. The *Sheffield Independent* of 3 January 1907 announced that:

> Arrangements were being made on January 16 1907 for speakers at the Montgomery Hall, Surrey Street, Sheffield which would consist of those suffragettes who had been imprisoned for their beliefs, as women who had already paid the penalty for their unique methods of bringing the claims of women to political enfranchisement.

Among the speakers were Miss Teresa Billington, who had been sent to prison on two previous occasions and Mary Gawthorpe, who was by now a familiar face in the city. The newspapers were still very disparaging about the meetings and despite the fact that the room had been reported to be three-quarters-full of women, the *Sheffield Independent* claimed that 'just a few of them had banded together to hear one or two of the daring, if somewhat misguided, speakers'. Another local reporter claimed that although the women on the platform were 'wreckers of other peoples' meetings' the only interruptions came from some of the babies brought by mothers who took the front seats in the hall. Miss Gawthorpe told her audience that 'You cannot have social reform of any kind unless you take into consideration the fact that women form half of the whole nation.' Mrs Edith Whitworth also encouraged more women to join the Sheffield WSPU and moved for a resolution demanding immediate legislation for the female franchise. Needless to say the *Sheffield Independent* dismally reported that 'several hundred misguided women voted for the resolution and only a handful dissented'.

Miss Mary Gawthorpe

Mary Gawthorpe, a regular speaker at Sheffield on female suffrage.

It was not only in Sheffield that more and more women were demanding the vote, and the WSPU were organising demonstrations in the capital city to which local women were invited. When no mention had been made in the Kings Speech of 1907 about female franchise, a demonstration was due to be held in London on 13 February to which women from other towns and cities had been invited to join. The previous day Edith Whitworth, a Mrs Yates from Pitsmoor and two other unnamed women were reported to be at the Sheffield railway station on their way to travel to London to attend. The four women were part of a large crowd estimated to be 800 strong which assembled

SHEFFIELD SUFFRAGETTES

Sheffield suffragettes at the station travelling to London to take part in demonstrations.

in front of the Houses of Parliament determined to bring the matter of female suffrage before the Prime Minister. The police were equally determined to break up the demonstration and it was alleged that they 'went into the women on mounted horses, driving them down streets and alleys'. As a result there were the arrests of thirty-four suffragettes including Mrs Whitworth and Mrs Yates. They had both been arrested as they tried to enter the House of Commons. The following day they were brought before the Westminster Police Court charged with disorder and given a fine of 10s or sent to prison for 14 days. Like other women before them they refused to pay the fine, and were then taken away to Holloway prison to complete their sentence.

Consequently on 27 February 1907 the two women were among others released from prison after serving their sentences. There to greet them, as they emerged through the gates of the prison at 8.30 a.m., was Mrs Pankhurst, Mrs Pethick Lawrence and a large assembly of other suffragettes accompanied by a brass band. A procession was formed and flags issued as the two Sheffield women joined the other protesters to march proudly along the Kingsway Road, and the Strand, where they were cheered vociferously as the band played 'See the Conquering Hero Comes'. Mrs Whitworth later described her experiences in prison and told a Sheffield reporter 'If you are not a rebel before going into Holloway, there is no reason to wonder at your being one when you come out.' Mrs Yates described how when they were arrested they were placed roughly in a prison van, where they had to sit huddled together for more than an hour. Both women insisted that they were not ashamed of being in prison for the cause and were quite ready to do the same again, although they both protested against the treatment they received in prison, but as Mrs Whitworth proclaimed:

> The authorities were very severe upon us. They did it to deter us from going again, but it certainly will not, for we are true daughters of the old Sheffield Chartists, and mean to fight, and if needs be, lay down our lives in the struggle.

The two women complained about prison food and the beds, which were simply plank beds with a thin mattress laid upon them, which were very uncomfortable. Mrs Yates also complained about the wardresses who were very officious in the way in which they dealt with the women. Although all the suffragettes were taken to church on Sundays in the morning and the afternoon, they were kept separate from all the other prisoners. Mrs Yates said that she shared a cell with five other 'comrades' and to pass away the time, they composed a new song for the suffragette cause. On 20 March 1907 yet another demonstration was held outside the House of Commons in

London in which another two Sheffield women, Mrs Jane Lockwood from the Darnall district and Mrs Annie Higgins from Walkley, were both arrested. Strongly criticised in court for their unwomanly behaviour, once again the two Sheffield women were given fourteen days imprisonment. When they were released on the morning of 4 April 1907 they too found a crowd of suffragettes waiting for them as well as a brass band. The whole group accompanied them as they made their way to a local restaurant for a celebratory breakfast. When both women returned back to their home city, they were described as looking none the worse for their experiences.

In February of 1908 the *Sheffield Independent* ran a poll to find out what the women of Sheffield thought about the suffragettes and their activities. On 8 February they announced that beginning the week of 10 February, a test poll would be held asking every women 'are you in favour of women having the vote?' The female head of every house would receive a voting paper on which she was to place a cross under 'yes' or

THE SHEFFIELD SUFFRAGETTES.

MRS. LOCKWOOD.   MRS. HIGGINS.

Mrs Jane Lockwood and Mrs Annie Higgins arrested for demonstrating outside the House of Commons in March 1907.

'no' accordingly. The second question asked 'do you approve of the methods of the suffragettes?' A reporter accompanied the canvasser in collecting the voting papers on 14 February and he found that many difficulties had been experienced, not by the women, but from their husbands. One housewife told him that she was very much in favour of the suffragettes and their activities, but her husband had made her sign against it, threatening to knock her down if she did not. Another husband, answering the door to the two men, told them that he had received the paper for his wife, but had burnt it, before slamming the door in their faces. At another house one ballot paper with a large cross in the 'no' column was also given and attached to it was a note which gave her reason. Signed simply from 'a working man's wife' the note read:

> My opinion of suffragettes is that if they were like some of us and had to try to pay 30s out of 20s, they would not have so much time to run about after votes for women. They ought to be in some of our shoes for a month, it would give them something else to think about.

When the results were analysed they found that 9,011 had voted in favour of women having the votes and 14,652 voted against, whilst 3,564 women approved of the methods of the suffragettes, 17,924 were not in favour. However, the results were seriously skewed, as obviously not all women had the freedom to answer those questions for themselves. Whether the men of the city were feeling threatened or not, a week later a suffragette meeting was seriously disrupted. The *Sheffield Evening Telegraph* announced on 20 February 1908 that Miss Adela Pankhurst was to speak at the Queen's Statue in Fargate. During her speech there were constant interruptions from a man singing a comic song refrain and other loud male hecklers. The process was becoming very boisterous when the police were called, and Miss Pankhurst was forced to leave at about 9.30 p.m. in a car, accompanied by cheers and jeers. Despite this the Sheffield suffragettes were not downhearted and instead used one of the politicians' own tactics

VOTES FOR WOMEN.
WOMEN'S SOCIAL AND POLITICAL UNION.
MEETING TO-NIGHT 8 p.m.
QUEEN'S STATUE.
MISS A. PANKHURST.

Meeting held by Adela Pankhurst at Queen Victoria's statue.

for meetings, with posters clearly labelled 'for women only' at their next WSPU meeting. These posters were clearly displayed at the Montgomery Hall on the evening of 25 March 1908 when over 1,000 women attended. Local newspapers printed a cartoon showing men being ejected from the hall. When it was also noted that many of the women in the audience were female teachers, the reporter from the *Sheffield Daily Telegraph* of 27 March 1908 dismissively stated, 'whether they hope the vote will enable them to reduce the pension age for teachers or compel all bachelors to marry before they are 30, has not yet been made clear'.

Despite the criticism the *Sheffield Independent* said that the meeting had 'provided the novelty of seeing the Montgomery Hall practically filled from floor to ceiling, with an audience of

SHEFFIELD SUFFRAGETTES.

Cartoon in Sheffield newspapers illustrating how reporters were now banned from attending suffragette meetings.

women'. Miss Adela Pankhurst introduced her sister Christabel who was said to be 'excelling as a cultured, graceful and effective speaker, who had a charm in her platform style'. She described to her audience the way in which the suffragettes had at first tried meek methods asking for a vote in the polite 'if you please' kind of way to begin with, but when this was ignored they resorted to an old maxim on which she had always been brought up, in that 'you might as well be killed for a sheep as a lamb'. Miss Christabel Pankhurst was described as an eloquent pleader of her cause, she was followed by Miss Gawthorpe who was accused of tending to 'harangue her audience as if she were addressing a street-corner meeting, instead of a company of educated ladies who had no intention of interrupting or brow beating the speaker'. But it was acknowledged that she never ceased to be interesting. Whatever the reporters' thoughts on the subject, it was clear that interest in the WSPU movement was fast growing in Sheffield.

On 29 October 1908 a demonstration of unemployed men marched on Sheffield which was hi-jacked by the Sheffield suffragettes. The men were intent on arriving at the Cutlers' Hall where the First Lord of the Admiralty, Mr Reginald McKenna had been invited to a feast. These occasions had been held every year for 285 years where notable men of influence were feted with a sumptuous meal, where no expense was spared. The demonstration of men were registering their disapproval at the fact that the opulence of the Hall and the food was flaunting the wealth when numbers of unemployed were starving in Sheffield. The scene was described in local newspapers as 'not for a long day has there been so much restlessness and hostility in evidence in Sheffield' as thousands of people congregating in the streets adjacent to the Cutlers' Hall. When the men marched towards the Hall they found a strong cordon of police barring their way. A council of war was held on Fargate, before proceeding to the Monument where inflammatory speeches were made. Meanwhile the suffragettes were also protesting against the visit of Mr McKenna, encouraged by the crowd. Miss Pankhurst and Mrs Edith Whitworth marched along Leopold Street intending to get to the entrance of the Cutlers' Hall, but they only got as far as a police cordon at the High Street, where a ninety-minute struggle ensued. During the debacle Adela and Edith Whitworth were very roughly handled by police constables. Adela told them 'I want to see Mr McKenna, I am going in, and I shall,' but she was politely told by Chief Inspector Hollis 'No, you're not going in, Miss Pankhurst.' Finally exhausted, the now perspiring women were forced to withdraw to the Town Hall, where Miss Pankhurst was seen to climb aboard a tram to the Moor. Meanwhile the numbers of unemployed men also continued to battle with police officers, but there were too many of them. Hoots and groans accompanied anyone stepping outside the Cutlers' Hall to the extent that the police were ordered to clear Church Street. During this time, Miss Pankhurst had disguised herself in dark clothes as a kitchen maid and, alone, she tried to get into the back door of the Hall along Fargate passage. Going up to one of the police officers she asked to speak to a Mrs Fletcher, who she said was assisting in the Hall. The first of the two officers did not recognise her, but another officer named Wood did, but before Miss Pankhurst could be arrested, she left undaunted. Miss Pankhurst returned to Sheffield the following year on 20 April 1909, where she spoke at a meeting held in the open air at the factory of Messrs Sanderson and Newbould. Ringing a hand bell to get their attention, Miss Pankhurst addressed a crowd of between 200–300 people on their lunch break. Unable to persuade the factory to lend her a dray to stand on, she addressed the crowd while hanging on precariously to an abutment at the base of a store house. Miss Pankhurst was remembered by some of the crowd, as one of those involved in the Albert Hall and the Cutlers' Hall demonstrations of a few months previously. She amused the crowd by stating that of course they were always thrown out of such meetings, but 'the more they were thrown out, the better it was for them as the newspapers would always make note of that, hence it supported their cause'. She was described as being a 'sprightly little leader who wore fashionable clothes', which it was suggested, 'provoked the envy of some of the factory lasses who formed part of her audience'. Although most of the crowd remained attentive there were some individuals who showed a disposition towards rowdiness, and three or four bad oranges and a couple of rotten eggs were thrown at her. Miss Pankhurst informed the crowd that, 'They had visited Liberal meetings and demanded votes for women, and refused to be put off. For as long as they kept quiet, they would never get any nearer the vote.'

She told the crowd that her mother was expected to arrive in Sheffield later that night, and would address another meeting in a few days time. The meeting in which her mother spoke was held three days later, at the Attercliffe Vestry Hall in the afternoon of 23 April 1909. Mrs Pankhurst spoke of the inequalities of laws which had been established by men, which affected women and children, without the consultation of any woman, who would see things quite differently. She also mentioned the coming elections to be held at Attercliffe and urged the voters of Sheffield to reject the Liberal nominee, Mr Lambert.

So determined were the women of Sheffield to keep out the Liberal candidate that at the entrance to every polling booth in Attercliffe on 4 May, a woman was placed urging people to vote against the government. Mrs Pankhurst kept her promise to return and was a visible presence during the proceedings 'flitting about the constituency all day in a motor car, gaily decorated with the colours of the WSPU'. The Women's Freedom League were also in attendance handing out cards which stated:

Attercliffe Division,
Sheffield, 4 May 1909

'To the Prime Minister,

Sir, I have this day voted against the Government nominee at the request of the women, as a protest against your attitude on the urgent question of votes for women. My vote would otherwise have been given for the Liberal candidate on this occasion.'

Yours truly

Voters were encouraged to sign the cards and forward them on to the prime minister. Altogether a total of 2,266 cards were forwarded as a fitting expression of the disgust that Sheffield female voters felt. They also collected over 5,000 signatures on a petition from electors also expressing their disgust at the stand taken by the government. In fact the Labour candidate, Mr Joseph Pointer, was elected for Attercliffe with more than 3,500 votes. Sadly, but true to form, it was announced in February 1914 that although Mr Pointer had said to the women 'If I win Attercliffe tonight, you women will have been responsible, and I shall see to it when I get to the House of Commons that I work for votes for women.' But, like many of his colleagues, once elected he did nothing!

Mr Pointer MP and women voters.

When the Prime Minister, Mr Herbert Asquith returned to Sheffield on the evening of 21 May 1909 it was probably with a sense of deep dread of the treatment he might have to endure at the hands of the Sheffield suffragettes. Nevertheless crowds of people had assembled outside the Edmund Road Drill Hall, Sheffield where he was due to appear. Once again, in an attempt to prevent disruptions, all women were banned from the meeting, and a six-foot high fence and a cordon of police had been erected to prevent them getting in. Before the meeting on 18 May 1909 it had been reported that:

> very little disguise is made of the fact that the organisers
> of the meeting are desperately afraid of the suffragettes,
> and the contest between the Liberal precautions and the
> suffragette wiliness will be regarded with great interest.
> Personally we should be inclined to put our money on
> the suffragettes, who have shown themselves no mean
> exponents of the gentle art of strategy.

The reporter was quite right, and they harangued Mr Asquith almost as soon as he arrived. When the prime minister's train

Edmund Road Drill Hall.

pulled up at the railway station one woman managed to get inside the barrier, where she shouted 'When are you going to give the votes to women Mr Asquith?' It was doubtful that he heard her due to the noise of the people gathered around him. What he could not fail to hear were the shouts throughout his journey along the streets of Sheffield, both on his way to the hotel and to the Drill Hall, of 'votes for women' and 'cowards, cowards'. The *Sheffield Independent* noted that 'there was not a woman present' inside the hall as Sir William Clegg told them 'the Liberals of Sheffield were determined that the mountebank methods of imported ladies should not be permitted to insult the Prime Minister'. Despite their precautions there had been some nasty scenes outside the Drill Hall as 'an attacking mob' tried to help the suffragettes in their efforts to storm the meeting. It was estimated that eight to ten thousand people had gathered, among whom were a large percentage of youths who had probably responded out of sheer curiosity and in anticipation of seeing the fun. Suddenly a command was given to the 150 police officers on duty as they drew their truncheons, and engaged in hand-to-hand fighting. One reporter climbed onto the roof of the hall to witness for himself the events unfolding below. He claimed that the conflict, which mainly took place in the Clough Road entrance to the Hall, was a result of the scheming of women to create riot and disorder. The reporter laid the blame directly onto the suffragettes who he reported 'fanned the flames', calling them nothing but 'hooligans'. However, the reality was that much of the disorder was caused by many of the mob, as they tried unsuccessfully to bodily lift some of the suffragettes over the six-foot high barricade. Using much violence the police pushed them back, time and time again. The unnamed reporter stated that these women used their fists and nails to such an extent that many of the officers had scratched faces and hands. Confronted by over 150 burly constables the suffragettes had little chance of defending themselves, as the officers wrestled with women much smaller than themselves. At one point the reporter disgustedly noted that he saw three hatless women, struggling with the police 'with their hair pulled down and hanging around their shoulders in a most disorderly fashion'. Helpless, these brave Sheffield women were dragged about in a manner that no self-respecting female should have to endure, and he gleefully was able to report that 'one of them had her clothes pulled up almost to her waist for the glory and dignity of womanhood'.

Unfazed by their inability to get inside the Hall, the Sheffield suffragettes held a meeting a short distance away and urged the crowd that had gathered around them to join them in storming the building. A woman later identified as a Miss Ainsworth told the crowd 'we call upon everybody to come along and follow us, and we will get into the hall and see Mr Asquith with your help'. They were unable to achieve what they set out to do though, as the police once more put up what was referred to as a Herculean effort. Biased as the reporter was in describing the melee between unarmed women and baton-wielding officers he concluded that 'under the most trying circumstances the police exercised exceptional tolerance, and while there were some vigorous bouts of fisticuffs, this was the only alternative to a baton charge for dealing with the roughs.'

He stated that he had it on good authority that their task the previous night was one of the most difficult accomplished within the memory of the oldest constables on the force.

The suffragette cause in Sheffield appeared to have moved up a notch in February of 1910 when Miss Adela Pankhurst arrived in the city to live at 45 Marlborough Road. She came at the invitation of Mrs Helen Archdale, a well-known figure in the suffragette movement. There the two women discussed using peaceful action to get the vote. Even though her mother and sister, Christabel, believed in militant action Adela and Helen Archdale initially wanted to continue by peaceful methods where possible. In order to do this they held regular Thursday 'at homes' on behalf of the Sheffield WSPU. They also acquired a shop at 26–28 Chapel Walk, Sheffield run by Miss Elsa Shuster, a woman who had herself spent fourteen days in prison for a stone throwing episode. They organised speeches by prominent suffragettes, Mrs Millicent Fawcett and Miss

45 Marlborough Road, Sheffield.

Muriel Matters of Australia at the Montgomery Hall, Sheffield. One of Miss Pankhurst's first meetings was to explain the latest developments of the movement to a gathering of about 100 local ladies in the drawing room of the Cutlers' Hall on the afternoon of 15 March 1910. She told them that Sheffield was now to be the centre of the WSPU which extended from Scarborough in the north, to Chesterfield in the south. Miss Pankhurst urged all the women of Sheffield to join them and reminded them that they could only rely on themselves to push forward for female suffrage. She pointed out that although there were 412 men in the House of Commons who had promised to support their campaign, not one of them had succeeded, despite their promises. Miss Pankhurst warned:

We are preparing our forces. We are not going to have any militant tactics until it is proved that we cannot get the vote any other way. Now is the time for women who don't like the military tactics to make them forever unnecessary. Prove that you are stronger than any government in the country and you will get the vote.

The women of Sheffield, like those of the rest of Britain were therefore jubilant in June 1910 when it was finally expected that the first Conciliation Bill introduced by David Shackleton would be pushed through Parliament on 9 June. It had contained over 250,000 signatures and an ecstatic meeting was held in Sheffield on June 8 where the *Sheffield Daily Telegraph* announced that 'the ladies are joyful, although they do their best to conceal their jubilation beneath a dignified exterior. They really do think that something is coming of the Shackleton Bill and that a million women will be enfranchised.' One speaker at the meeting ecstatically stated that:

it is difficult to see how further concessions can be refused. If the Shackleton Bill is passed, we shall initiate a revolution the end of which it is a little difficult to discern. Whether it will go inexorably on until King George V summonses his first Petticoat Government is a matter the future alone can decided.

Despite the bill being passed in the House of Commons, it was dropped when it was announced that another election would take place in November. Suffragettes all over Britain were furious and at that point it was decided in Sheffield that they had no option but to step up their campaign of violence. A mass rally of over 60,000 people for women's suffrage had been arranged to be held in Kensington on 18 June 1910 and the Sheffield suffragettes headed for London to take part in the procession taking with them their new banner, which was described as being a 'fine piece of work'. When they arrived in London they joined other women marching together and the sight was spectacular. One elderly man who stood watching, told a reporter that he had never seen so many petticoats in his life. Those suffragettes who had served time in prison for their beliefs proudly carried broad arrows as they marched.

In November 1910 another Conciliation Bill made it to the second reading, but ran out of time. In response the WSPU protested and over 200 women were assaulted and manhandled in London as they attempted to break through the ranks of police. Although the heavy-handed police tactics had already been seen in Sheffield, there was a general outcry at the demonstrations of brutality in the capital. The government tried to ban newspaper pictures of the attacks, but there was no hiding the heavy-handed methods that the police used on the women. The suffragettes were outraged and the day was called 'Black Friday'. Following this, Mrs Emmeline Pankhurst declared that increasingly militant tactics would now be used in order to gain the franchise for women. No longer would gentle persuasion be used and she incited each woman to take whatever rebellious action they could in order to achieve their purpose. The women of Sheffield were equally determined to do their part. They decided that the best method of action was by damaging pillar boxes containing letters and parcels using 'bombs' consisting of any noxious substances which would accomplish this purpose. On 7 December 1912 the *Sheffield Daily Telegraph* reported that 'the latest mania which has spread like some noisome epidemic through the ranks of the militant suffragists, has now spread to Sheffield'. It was recorded that the previous night a raid had been made on several pillar boxes about the city, which had corrosive material poured onto the letters waiting for collection inside. Referring to the perpetrators as 'petticoated hooligans' the reporter stated that:

> If anyone in Sheffield had held any lingering doubts as to the unfitness of women for the suffrage, last night's insane outrage must surely have dissipated them. It is undeniably hard on the law abiding suffragettes to be tarred with the odium of the militant fraternity. They

have indeed only one course open to them, and that is to postpone their claim to the vote until the Maenads of the movement, insignificant in numbers, and in many cases hired at so much a week to do their dirty work, mend their methods and their manners.

It was announced on 7 October 1911 that Miss Adela Pankhurst had suffered a breakdown in her health and a decision had been taken, against her will that she would stand down as organiser in Sheffield. Despite the fact that her stay in Sheffield had been so brief, she was long remembered by the Sheffield people. The following year a 21-year-old woman, Molly Murphy applied and she quickly realised that her job was not only organising meetings, but working in the shop, chalking slogans on the pavements, selling copies of *The Suffragette* and arranging 'at homes' to which all classes were invited. Murphy was also responsible for organising open air meetings, many of these being held at Queen Victoria's jubilee statue outside the Town Hall (now in Endcliffe Park). The statue rested on granite steps which were a convenient platform for orators of the period. Murphy felt this was a very appropriate place as the Queen 'typified in her outlook, almost every aspect of womanhood of which we were now in revolt'.

In her book *Molly Murphy: Suffragette and Socialist*, she describes how she and Miss Schuster arrived home in the early hours of the morning, after a night chalking slogans in the streets, and on the walls of various buildings in Sheffield. Murphy described the city of Sheffield in 1912 as:

Crowded trams, double deckers and single deckers with their thousands of passengers rolled to and fro between masses of blackened red bricked houses to blackened factories. I can still see young boys tired and almost asleep on the trams going to work and the town as the rumble of machinery was incessant and the night skies aglow from the fires of blast furnaces. The armour plated mills thundered at all hours of the day and night.

Sign erected outside 45 Marlborough Road.

On 31 January 1913 the tactics of the militant suffragettes were again condemned by the *Sheffield Daily Telegraph*. From the one or two pillar boxes which had been attacked previously, damage on a much larger scale was now being reported in the centre and the west of the city. Five pillar boxes in Moor Oaks

Statue of Queen Victoria, now in Endcliffe Park.

Road, West Street, Division Street, Glossop Road and Surrey Street had all been attacked, by pouring some black/green ink or quick-drying black varnish over the contents. Once again it was reported that the damage had not been extensive and the post officer workers were able to deliver all the correspondence to the correct addresses. It was estimated that the attack had been carried out between 8 p.m. and 9.30 p.m. the previous night. No arrests were made, but constables were stationed near some of the boxes in the city throughout the following nights. Molly Murphy admitted to joining in with the outrages in her book as she described how she and Miss Schuster went to London to pick up some of these 'bombs' before placing them in letter boxes around the city. On one occasion she had someone take charge of the shop on Chapel Walk, so that she could slip several of these bombs inside the large pillar box outside the Town Hall. Acting as if posting letters, she claimed:

> Contrary to expectations, in that some time was meant to elapse before they fired, I had only walked a few yards away when smoke came belching out of the box. At the same time a car backfired in the street and people thought a bomb had exploded. The fire brigade came dashing up and a crowd gathered round. I mixed with the crowd and looked on.

A police detective stood beside Murphy as they watched the people milling about and he said sympathetically 'We know its the London lot that do this kind of thing, Miss Murphy, and not you young ladies. I wish all people were like you.' Little did he realise her part in the attack.

By 4 February 1913 the Sheffield suffragettes were determined to let people know where they stood. The *Sheffield Daily Telegraph* reported that several notices had been erected at various sites across the city. The women were now appealing to others to resort to lawlessness if it was required. The notices read:

DEFY AND RESIST GOVERNMENT
'Oyez! Oyez! Oyez! Dare to be free!

'Whereas the Prime Minister has egregiously failed to secure the fulfilment of his pledges, militant suffragists who henceforward will require nothing short of a Government measure for the enfranchisement of women, announce their intention to defy and resist government without consent, and invite the people of this country to rally to their support.' Given in the year of our Lord 1913 (January).

The bombing attacks on pillar boxes continued and on 15 April 1913 a double box on Surrey Street was attacked, which was important as it was largely used for the correspondence from the Town Hall. A description of the discovery of the damage was reported in the local newspapers the following morning. It stated that at about 3.45 p.m. smoke was seen emanating from the box and information was given to the Sheffield Fire Brigade. It was thought that the letters were smouldering and a fire brigade official was sent to obtain the keys of the box. Inside they found two small phials, wrapped in paper containing acid, but only three envelopes had been damaged, although the addresses were still decipherable. A crowd began to assemble and watched as the police and fire brigade officials dealt with the matter. Although other reports of damaged pillar boxes were heard throughout the city, no serious damage resulted. It was reported the next day that several plain-clothes policemen were seen in the vicinity of letter boxes in the principal thoroughfares of Sheffield, although their vigilance was largely unrewarded. One day later there was retaliation in Sheffield when some 'strong sticky fluid' was poured through the letter box of the office at Chapel Walk. Thankfully no other damage had been done and the situation was discovered the following morning.

The fact that little damage had been done resulted in a more determined attempt on 22 April 1913, on a particular box standing on the High Street near to the Church gates. It was estimated that as many as 200 letters had been destroyed, by an uncorked bottle containing oil and ink. The fluid had dripped through the large pile of letters and was emanating from the bottom of the letter box onto the pavement when the postman arrived for the midnight collection. When the news that the bombing of a letter box at the High Street had taken place in the city, so large a crowd had gathered at the entrance to the Parish Church, that for twenty minutes or more they were instructed to move on by police officers. So when another of these 'bombs' were found at the Park branch library on 27 May 1913 the *Sheffield Daily Telegraph* indignantly reported that the attack had been carried out 'on unoffending friends and foe alike, and that sanctuary is not even to be found in the quiet precincts of the public libraries of the city'.

It seems that a reader using the library had noticed a parcel which had been left on a landing near the reading room. The parcel, on which was written 'Votes for Women', was quickly dunked into a pail of water and allowed to become fully saturated before it was finally opened. A detective was soon on the scene and he found that it contained a number of firework cartridges. These were attached to lengthy fuses and an arrangement of wires, the purpose of which was reported to be hard to detect. There was also a considerable quantity of gunpowder, paraffin and chemicals. The police took charge of the bomb, but the person who left it was never identified.

News was being reported from London on the force-feeding of suffragettes imprisoned for their beliefs. As a consequence, on 13 May 1914 a deputation of Sheffield WSPU gathered before the Bishop of Sheffield, Leonard Burrows claiming that such inhuman treatment was nothing less than torture. The bishop was informed that the women were not being force-fed through concerns of their health, as it had been applied to women who had only been in custody for twenty-four hours. Despite this, force-feeding was imposed on them three times a day. The bishop suggested that it might have been made more difficult due to the women's struggles, but Miss Shuster told him that struggling was a reflex action of the body, due to the excruciating pain which was being inflicted. The deputation left after the bishop promised to look further into the matter, but before he could take any effective action it was announced that the country was in a state of war. On 4 August 1914 suffragettes all over Britain laid down their struggle. The Women's Freedom League leaflet 'The Vote' summarised the suffragettes' position at that moment in time. It stated that 'they feel keenly the situation of the Country at the present moment and consequently have decided to abstain during the war from all forms of active militancy'.

So it was all over, and the records show that Sheffield women who had made up the suffragette movement, now poured all their energy into winning the war by whatever means were available to them. There is little doubt, however, that they would find it difficult to go back to the confinement of their previously domestic lives. For many years they had found a freedom of breaking away from patriarchal authority, to establish a movement where strong women bonded together for a common aim. Now they were expected to watch their men leave to go and fight, whilst they busied themselves doing ordinary tasks undertaken by women in wartime. Little research has been done into the thoughts and feelings of these women, but I have no doubt that they were greatly disappointed. How did Sheffield women like Edith Whitworth, Jane Lockwood, Annie Higgins and the woman only known as Mrs Yates feel about going back to their ordinary lives? They had served sentences in Holloway Prison for their strong beliefs in equality for women, how could they passively go back to the only role left to them of being wives and mothers? The truth of the matter is that we shall never know, but what is on record is the fact that the women of Sheffield threw themselves behind supporting the war effort, and heroically supporting their husbands and sons in any way they could.

CHAPTER SEVEN

Sheffield Women and the First World War

When the outbreak of war was announced on 4 August 1914 not many people in Britain had a concept of how it would affect those left at home. The first few weeks were caught up in the arrangements for the mobilization of troops, and for the women who remained behind their immediate concern was naturally one of finances, and how they would manage with their husbands and sons away at the front. The government quickly arranged for families of enlisted soldiers and sailors to have a separation allowance which was a portion of their relative's pay. A week later they were requesting that upon enlistment all men were to have with them their marriage certificate, and birth certificates for all the children, in order that separation allowances could be issued. Finally it was agreed by March 1915 that fighting men's wives would receive a separation allowance of 12*s* 6*d* a week, 17*s* 6*d* for a wife with one child, and 21*s* for a wife with two children plus 2*s* 6*d* a week for each extra child. Relief Committees were quickly formed in Sheffield to ensure that no local families would suffer any immediate destitution. Nevertheless the speed with which the men of the city were enlisted meant that the women in charge of the local branch of the Soldiers' and Sailors' Families Association (SSFA) were inundated with requests. So many enquiries were made that the offices were moved from Church House, Sheffield to the larger Lower Montgomery Hall in Surrey Street where emergency payments could be made. Initially the government intended to pay the allowance on a monthly basis, but the SSFA were urgently requesting that payment be made weekly.

To complicate matters some of the wives of the fighting men had been awarded an extra allowance from their previous employers for the duration of the war, whilst others had not. The unfairness of this situation was brought to the attention of the local newspapers in a letter to the editor of the *Sheffield Daily Telegraph* on 13 March 1915. The writer pointed out that:

> We still have to live and pay the same price for our food. My husband is a soldier but I am not receiving any allowance from the works where he was employed, yet I still have to live and pay my way as best as I can out of it.

By September 1915, the cost of separation payments to relatives left at home was still a subject of discontent for the women of the city. One such letter signed by 'A WIFE' complained that she now had to manage on 12*s* 6*d* a week, but before the outbreak of hostilities her husband had been earning 9*s* a day at his employment which he had given up to enlist. She stated that even though he had already served for many years as 'an old soldier who had done his bit', he had joined up again as he thought it was his duty to do so. Because of the pittance given by the government, he had been obliged to pay his wife some extra money out of the small amount he was receiving. The writer added that if she had been a young woman she would have been able to find a job, but she classed herself as an 'old one, with an invalid to look after'.

Perhaps the biggest impact on wives of the city made at this time was the development of a Sheffield branch of the National Union of Women Workers (NUWW) in 1914. This was an organisation which had been set up in 1895, initially to respond to the inequalities of working women, but by the outbreak of the First World War it moved into the concerns facing women in society at large. In Sheffield the NUWW were instrumental in setting up a social group under the auspices of a Women's War Club in the city in order to support wives of enlisted servicemen. The Lady Mayoress announced in January 1915 that steps were being taken to acquire premises in Pond Street, near to the post office which had previously been a grocery store. The premises which rose over three storeys were in a particularly good position for women who used to queue at the post office to collect their separation allowance every Monday. The Club, which unofficially opened on 25 March 1915, was open every day from 10 a.m. to 10 p.m., where women were encouraged to meet together with other army and navy wives and families for mutual support. They were encouraged to write to their relatives, or there was a warden on duty who could write letters for those unable to do so themselves. There was also a sewing machine for the use of women who needed it, and all for a subscription of 2d a month. The top floor of the building was shared between the caretakers' apartments and a nursery, which was described as being 'stocked with dolls' houses, a rocking horse and toys of all descriptions'. The second floor was a spacious club room furnished with a piano, a sideboard, a sofa, chairs and tables and all sorts of newspapers and writing materials as well as the nucleus of a library. The bottom floor held a kitchen and a serving hatch which led into a restaurant opening onto the street. There was even entertainment provided which consisted of patriotic recitations, songs and dancing. Throughout

Wives and dependents of our troops at the front, waiting in queue at the General Post Office, Sheffield, yesterday, to draw War Office separation allowance.

Women queuing to collect separation allowance.

Interior of one of the rooms of the Sheffield Women's War Club, situate in Pond Street, near the Post Office. The club is a new venture of the Sheffield Branch of the National Union of Women Workers, and is intended as a place where women may meet to encourage and hearten one another, and find rest, recreation, and help.

The comfortably furnished second floor of the War Club Sheffield.

the years of the war the Club also ran a series of lectures on cookery and the needs of children for the wives and mothers that attended. The Club was so successful that by January 1916 the Sheffield Women's War Club had 500 members with a daily attendance of forty to fifty service wives.

Perhaps the most significant formation which the NUWW had in the city of Sheffield was in the women's patrols which they established across Britain. At the outbreak of the war Sheffield town council, among others, were getting worried about the morals of the young girls who were alleged to be 'khaki crazy' at the sight of young men in uniforms in their city. Also there were concerns about young men seducing vulnerable girls, and the answer appeared for a group of local women to patrol parks and city streets where young people congregated at night. If they found any young couples together in the dark they were to try to turn them away into some more wholesome recreations. In March 1915 the Mayor, Councillor Oliver C. Wilson announced that the Lady Mayoress was interested in forming a group of women willing to volunteer to patrol the city's streets and parks at night. He asked that any women interested should forward their name to the Town Hall. These women patrols would volunteer to spend two hours, twice a week and would patrol in pairs, although they carried no authority and had no powers of arrest. His offer was quickly taken up and on 29 March 1915 it was announced that twenty-four Sheffield women had now officially been recognised by the military and police authorities, and were ready to start their work in the city. These patrols were placed under the supervision of a Patrol Leader called Miss Margaret Firth. The following month it was announced that twenty-five more women had been enrolled, and were at that time being trained and instructed in the duties they would have to perform. The local newspapers described how these women could soon be seen on the streets of Sheffield. They wore a blue-and-white band on their left arm, bearing the letters NUWW with the registered number of the patrol underneath. The women would also carry a card authorising them by Sheffield chief constable. By November it was announced that the volunteers had spoken to 550 local girls and induced them to join clubs and classes in which to take the young men, instead of roaming the streets unsupervised at night. One of the regulations was that these patrols would not try to separate couples, but endeavour to speak to the girl on her own, in a friendly way.

By October 1917 Miss Margaret Firth left to take up another position, but she told a meeting of the NUWW on 19 October that in the previous eighteen months, six districts had been regularly patrolled, and she had sent in monthly reports to the chief constable of Sheffield. Miss Firth closed her report by giving thanks to the local women who had tirelessly given their support. The NUWW stated that the work had been so important that they 'continued to hope for a force of professional women police who could render a similar useful service in Sheffield'. The following week the subject was picked up by a local reporter who stated that he had no idea that such patrols existed in the city. He said that he recollected that a suggestion had been made a while ago in Sheffield, but as he had heard no more he thought that the subject had lapsed for lack of interest. Instead he was astonished to hear that these women had accomplished such useful work, although he admitted that they were few in number and therefore their activities had been limited. The reporter was informed that the patrols were also extremely useful in monitoring public houses where young people gathered to drink and cause mischief. Other patrols regularly visited railway stations dealing with young girls who went there for amusement, or to prevent women trying to importune soldiers or sailors returning home on leave. By January 1918, the women patrols were being supervised by Mrs H.F. Hall and so useful had their work been, that the Commissioner of Police had decided to employ them as auxiliaries to the Sheffield police force. There were at that time eighty-four women patrols, who were supplied with greatcoats and their expenses were paid out of police funds. Others were being employed specifically as park keepers, to supervise young people using the parks to do their courting. Sadly by the end of the war the patrols were found to be no longer necessary and a decision was made to dispense with their services.

Throughout the war years Sheffield women were most anxious to do their utmost for the war effort. Women who had their own family commitments and were unable to do more practical work, might involve themselves in ensuring comforts for wounded soldiers who were recovering from their injuries. Donations of eggs, sausages, boiled bacon, homemade cakes, tinned fruit and ham were regularly collected and delivered to the military hospitals. More practical gifts of pyjamas, tooth brushes and dressing gowns were also very welcome. Other women who were unable to leave the house due to family commitments, were encouraged to knit socks and balaclavas for the men at the front. These were to be delivered to the 'Personal Comforts for Wounded Soldiers' depot in Leopold Street, Sheffield. Some women took to the task so energetically that a letter was sent to the editor of the *Sheffield Independent* dated 27 November 1915 which included a plea for the knitting of garments to be banned at concerts. The letter signed from

'SOCKS FOR SOLDIERS' began by saying that the writer was not an old fossil, but a young man who was protesting against the women:

> who make it impossible for anyone to follow the artistic work of famous interpreters of masterpieces, owing to their overweening desire to show how industrious they are. Because of these clickers of knitting needles, little could be heard and there is no reason why other people should be annoyed. I suggest that a line on the programme for the next concert should say 'No Knitting Allowed'. Yours etc.

Those who were able to sew were asked to make other items for the soldiers at the front. The *Sheffield Independent* of 15 August 1915 announced that their 'Lady Editor' would now supply patterns for garments needed by the troops and encouraged women to 'stitch, stitch, stitch'. The reporter stated that:

> ...every stitch is a prayer that all war may end, and is executed in the sure and certain hope that our soldiers and sailors, who brave the enemies' assaults and who suffer such injuries as may necessitate hospital treatment, shall have ready to hand such comforts as will make for a speedy recovery.

When another consignment of comforts was needed in July 1915 it was reported that Miss Edith Sorby, the Hon. Sec. of the depot would personally be at the hospital stores to receive gifts. Not only was she asking for practical gifts, but also sticks, rubber tips for crutches, cotton slings, summer socks etc. She requested that these were urgently needed at the Base hospital, the Infirmary, Winter Street and Woffinden Hospital. The newspaper commented that 'Sheffield and the wide district covered by us, will not have reason to be other than proud of the manner in which its womenfolk have responded to the national bugle call for help.' Women were also encouraged to send their own parcels for the men at the front, and the newspaper offered their own premises as a collection point 'from which gifts could be passed to brothers, sisters and sweethearts'. The following week it was reported that every available foot of office space held groups of people collecting gifts for the troops, and as a result the first consignment of bulky packages were on their way.

Before long though, Sheffield women were proving useful in other areas. One unnamed person recognised early in the war the useful nature to which women would soon be able to play a part. A letter appeared in the columns of a local newspaper dated 9 January 1915, whose writer stated that there was in the city many expert lady clerks and typists who were out of work. Nevertheless he stated that the Clerks Association was swamped with applications for male clerks, which was impossible to fill as the majority needed were of military age. He asks:

> Why cannot these posts be filled by ladies, who would willingly agree to take them temporarily until the war was over? I think if the leader of the Town Council would consider this matter, as other towns have done, there would be a greater reduction on the labour books and registers.

Others wanted to take on a more important role, so when it was announced that a convalescent home was to be opened in Sheffield, there were plenty of local women anxious to sign up to become nurses. In February 1915 it was announced that the Duke of Rutland had kindly agreed to place a part of Longshaw Lodge at the disposal of the government for this very purpose. This was a shooting lodge which had been built in 1827, just seven miles north of the city, which now provided a restful setting for those men wounded in the war. The news was announced by the Mistress Cutler who invited local women to join her Voluntary Aid Detachment (VAD) unit. The new nurses would be under the direction of a trained nurse, who would be appointed to support them. Many of the local women signed up and they were most interested to hear about the position of nurses serving at the front, which was the subject of a lecture

Wounded soldiers getting plenty of fresh air in outside beds.

given by Miss S. Macnaughton at the Albert Hall in Sheffield. The lecture on 25 June 1915 was to an audience consisting of employees of Messrs Cammell, Laird and Co. and their wives. Miss Macnaughton told the audience about her experiences at the front in Belgium at midnight on 7 October 1914, at Antwerp. The staff, who were working in a large concert hall which had been transformed into a hospital, were told that they expected to be bombarded by the Germans. The nurses were given the choice of leaving, although none of them did so. She described how the bombardment started and the noise was horrendous, but the nurses just bustled about saying to everyone 'now we are not going to leave you'. She said how it made her laugh to think that a handful of women could pretend to protect a lot of wounded men against the shells, and yet it really did calm the patients. Some of the injured were taken into the coal cellars where the nurses spent the night caring for them, and despite the heaviness of the shelling, even the younger nurses showed no fear. When at last she left Antwerp she stated that it was so sad to see beautiful residences burning in the empty streets, with no one to stop the flames.

Other women, who did not wish to take up nursing, were looking around to see where they could offer their service and so there was a certain amount of relief on 17 March 1915 when the War Service Register encouraged all women who wanted to find work to give their names. As a result the following day over 5,000 application forms were issued from all classes of local women, anxious to release those men who were still employed to be free to enlist. They worked as tram conductors, porters and in clerical positions. Within a few days an advertisement for women conductors was to be seen in the local newspapers. The Sheffield Tramway Department stated that they needed women over the age of 25 who would be paid 16s a week, and they would be provided with a cap and coat, but the women had to supply their own dark skirts. Ten Sheffield women started on the Walkley to Firth Park and Walkley to Intake routes on 8 June 1915 and the interest of the passengers using the trams was instantly noted. A reporter stated that 'the courageous and confident, but becoming way in which the bulk of them tackled their task was distinctly credible'. It was intended to train up new women every week, until the required number had been employed. Now these conductors could be seen around the city in their uniforms of plain blue serge and hats of straw in the 'boater' style. The scheme was so successful that by later that year in October 1915 an article was written in the *Sheffield Independent* which stated that the sight of lady conductors was no longer a novelty in the city and they had now become a 'war institution'. At that time it was estimated that more than 300 women had been recruited as female conductors. Some were then undertaking training, whilst others were already at work doing split shifts, and the whole scheme was deemed to be one of the great successes of the Great War. The reporter said that: 'On every hand there is evidence that the patrons of the Sheffield trams appreciate the coming of the women. As conductors they are courteous gentle and very humane and, not least of all, businesslike and efficient.'

FEMALE TRAM CONDUCTOR IN SHEFFIELD.

The female tram conductor in Sheffield has been duly installed. On a Walkley-Intake route car one was photographed yesterday.

Sheffield female conductor in uniform in Sheffield during the First World War.

Mr A.R. Fearnley the General Manager of the Tramways Department added his own comments, which seemed to exhibit some surprise that the women of Sheffield had done so well. He admitted that they looked for success, but added that 'our expectations have been exceeded, and both the training and the actual carrying out of the work had been much easier than expected'. The reporter asked him if the women were standing up to the 'wear and tear' of the role, and he replied that there had been no sign that they were suffering in any way from the physical strain of the work. In order to combat the cold winter months though, in addition to the blue serge uniforms, they were to be outfitted with waterproof coats, a long blue cloth overcoat and a waterproof hat. He concluded that the women were doing ordinary men's duties in almost every section of the department.

Sheffield women were also proving themselves invaluable in many diverse employment opportunities in the city by August 1916. As well as conductors, it was noted that they were now working as tool makers, gardeners, bank clerks, postmen, letter sorters, porters and carriage cleaners. It would seem that there was little work that local women could not do. That same month a firm in Sheffield was reported to have taken on women to work in the brickyards, making and packing bricks. In Woodseats there were twenty women employed delivering the post, and the first half dozen had been employed in the Sheffield Post Office in the Telegraph department. Towards the end of the war it was found that many skilled female telegraphists had eventually enlisted into the signal service of the Royal Engineers. Better educated girls and women of the city were now also busy working as bank clerks, working from 9 a.m. to 5 p.m. with a starting wage of £1 a week. For many women and young girls this was the first time that they had experienced any financial independence, nevertheless the expectation was clearly understood that when the men returned from the front they would have to leave their employment.

One of the biggest industries to employ Sheffield women was in the steelworks which now provided munitions for the war. As early as 1915 there was already a shell crisis which meant that many local firms had turned their businesses to the provision of all articles made from steel, such as guns, shells, body armour, bayonets, explosives, airplanes and grenades. Sheffield steelworks such as Hadfield's Steel Foundry Co., John Brown, Cammell Laird & Co. and Thomas Firth & Sons now turned from steel production to munitions. Hundreds of Sheffield women looking for jobs were enlisted into these works which unlike other factory work, was seen as morally acceptable for women because it aided the war effort. By June 1915 applications for munitions workers were so intense, that clerks

WOMEN'S WORK IN MUNITION FACTORIES.

Female munitions workers during the First World War.

were kept busy from its commencement to finish. On 25 June 1915, an advert appeared in the local newspapers which stated 'Get into the Factory and Supply the Firing Line' and before long the women were working day and night shifts, sometimes undertaking a fifty-six hour week.

By January 1916 the firm of Thomas Firth & Sons opened the National Projectile Factory at Templeborough, and many workers arrived at Sheffield to fill some of the 5,700 positions needed. The girl machinists were divided up into gangs for which they were paid piece work and each gang was supervised by a girl charge hand, who received a set rate plus a bonus. Some of these charge hands were simply untrained women who were wives and relatives of the management, it being naturally assumed that as middle-class they were automatically suited to a supervisory role. The workforce were not totally composed of women as there were a certain number of highly skilled male workers, to teach the girls how to manipulate the tools and to keep them in good order. What is often ignored in reporting about women munitions workers is the attitude of these male workers towards them in the workplace, which was not always encouraging and supportive. The fact was that many of these men resented women encroaching on their territory and using their machines. The *Sheffield Independent* illustrated this opposition on 3 March 1916, when five male munitions workers refused to work with a woman worker. They were brought before the chair of the Sheffield Munitions Court, Sir William Clegg and one of the men named Morley spoke for the others. He told the chair that he did not refuse to work, but did not want to work with a woman. Sir William asked him what business it was of his, if the manager appointed a woman to do the job. Morley explained that they had moved him off the machine he had worked at for a long time and had put her on it. A representative from the projectile factory told the court that the men had objected to the woman being put on one of the lathes, and as a consequence a man called Athey had been summarily dismissed. In retaliation the men had worked so slowly that they had held up the output. The representative explained that in two hours on the day of the dispute they had completed only four shells, which really only took twenty-seven minutes each and therefore such delays could not be warranted. The men were fined 20*s* each, apart from the youngest who was only 14 who was let off with a warning. Many other men felt the same, but the need for the women munitions worker was so imperative that they simply had to put up with it.

Despite the fact that women munitions workers were urgently needed they were still not paid at the same rate as the men. In April 1915 there had been a meeting of the NUWW in the Montgomery Hall, Sheffield where a resolution was made and carried with the best of intentions. The resolution stated: 'That this meeting of the National Union of Women Workers urges all women entering an industry to become members of a trade union, and demand equal wages for equal work, especially those working for the war period.'

At least that was the theory, but in the real world women were still paid a lot less than men. Councillor Alf Barton stated in June 1915 that at a large Sheffield armament works, where it had been understood that women would earn 16*s* to 18*s* a week, they were actually working for 8*s*. He also spoke of another woman who had been sent to a job working in the cutlery industry where she was offered 12*s* a week. She was promptly informed by the men at the works that if she accepted that wage, it would be very unpleasant for her. The woman, afraid of reprisals, refused the job.

In March 1917 the National Projectile Factory of Thomas Firths introduced a works magazine called *The Bombshell*. The magazine was designed to use both propaganda and humour in order to unite the male and female workers, indeed so proud were the editors of the magazine that a copy was sent to HM The Queen and Winston Churchill, then Minister for Munitions. Despite the magazine's patriotic idealism, it displayed a very patronising attitude towards the women workers. For example on the page dedicated to 'Things We Want to Know' one of the questions was 'how many hours each week in aggregate, are spent by feminine members of staff in doing their hair?' Throughout the magazine was an acknowledgement that the employment of women was seen only as a temporary necessity, and they would be expected to gratefully return to their homes once the men came home. This message was given in the Christmas issue of 1917 from the works manager's wife, Mrs Kay, who wrote specifically to all the women workers. She said:

> Many of you have left your homes and children to the tender mercy of others, and return home at night to find much anxiety in addition to hard work at the factory [...] After the war many will be glad to return to the home and the old sphere in which women wield their highest influence.

One of the most heart warming reports in the magazine, however, was the way in which the workers reacted to the news that the war was finally over. The 'Victory Edition' for November 1918 reported that a cry of 'war's o'er, lasses' rang throughout the factory and immediately the women all downed their tools and switched off their machines. Some sang, some hugged and some kissed before rushing outside to see the flag hoisted. Then there was a general stampede for the canteen where foremen climbed up into the rafters and sat there to hear the official proclamation. Despite the celebrations, there were the sad faces of those who had lost relatives and friends in the war among the happy cheering throng. When it was announced that there would be 'no more work today, girls' the women needed no second telling. The report apologised to the poor conductresses in the tramcars, who were nearly driven frantic at the singing and general hilarity which continued all the way into the city centre. Once the war was over, the firm of Thomas Firth & Sons moved to Norfolk Works where new editions of *The Bombshell* could still be bought. Once again the roles of the now departed women workers were put back in their place, as it reported: 'Now that the female shell workers have served the useful purpose for which they were enlisted, and more men being available for present requirements, the old order may be reverted to as occasion demands and the female substitute displaced.'

The Bombshell also reported on the activities of the firm's sports team which included a women's hockey and football teams who practised on the sports field which adjoined the factory. The Christmas edition of 1917 included a report on the football game which the women's team lost to the Empire Mills Team from Barnsley by seven goals to nil. The report stated that 'our girls must learn to pass the ball to the wings more, instead of kicking it straight out in front of them'.

Many local firms including Thomas Firth's, had encouraged sports to improve the fitness of their workers. These had originally started as teams of munitions women played against each other for charity. At first women football teams were seen as a curiosity and an amusing entertainment, rather than a serious challenge to yet another male dominated sport. But the increase in attendances at these games quickly escalated. Such a one was reported in April 1917 when shell hands and shell rollers from the National Projectile Factory raised £6.15*s* towards war funds. It was estimated that as many as 2,000 people had turned up to watch the match. Nevertheless the game had its detractors. The *Sheffield Independent*'s 'Women's Topics' column claimed that playing the game was unsuitable for the gentler sex and stated that it was injurious to the female frame. The reporter concluded that the ability to kick a ball hard enough would damage a woman's legs and prophesying that 'they will regret it when their football days are over'. Other opinions suggested that indulging in such activities would result in women's reproductive organs being damaged. This prejudice continued long after the war had finished when many of the former munitions workers continued to play football. In May 1921 thousands once again turned up to watch when the famous Dick Kerr's International Ladies Football Club of Preston played the Atlanta Ladies of Huddersfield at Sheffield. On that day the crowd was estimated to have held over 53,000 supporters. The Lady Mayoress of Sheffield attended the match and although she commented that the sport was 'good exercise for girls', others disagreed and thought the game was too unladylike. One of these included eminent medical specialists, such as an unnamed Harley Street specialist who stated in 1921 that:

> members of the medical profession generally are distinctly opposed to the idea of women and girls playing a game, which for them has serious and well known risks and dangers, without any of the corresponding balance of advantages. Football is far too rough and tumble a game for it to be for a moment considered suitable for either women or girls.

Another prestigious organisation which condemned the women's football teams and also thought it was unladylike and unsuitable, was able to do something about it. In December 1921 the *Sheffield Independent* reported that the Football Association had requested all football clubs to refuse the use of grounds for games involving women footballers. Despite such attempts to sabotage female football players, the enthusiasm for the game remained and Sheffield women's teams continued to play on other venues. In August 1929 a female football match was played at the Steel Products ground at Templeborough at

6.14 p.m. when the Ladies Cricketers and Footballers teams met the Darwin's Ladies Cricketers and Footballers. The crowd of about 500 spectators saw the Carbrook team beat the Darwin team by nine goals. The following year the Carbrook team played the Sheffield United Women's football section at which over 1,000 supporters watched the game to see Carbrook team beat them by two goals to one. Despite the high attendances at such matches the Football Association refused permission for the Sheffield women's football team to be played at Derby. They stated that 'it ought not to be encouraged' and the application was refused. Nevertheless the games continued to be played for charity on other community fields and continued to attract large crowds.

There is little doubt therefore that Sheffield women stepped up to do what was needed for the city during the war. However, a more shameful episode took place in Sheffield when rioting against German people broke out, following the sinking of the *Lusitania*. For the victims, many of whom had lived peacefully in Sheffield for many years, they found it incredible that such violence could be shown towards them. On 14 May 1915 large groups of women, girls and young boys attacked shops in Attercliffe belonging to those shopkeepers who sounded like they had a German name or had any German connections. This strange 'patriotism' was possibly encouraged by looters, as in most cases pork butchers were an especial target, and following the attacks many women were seen carrying away sides of pork, ham and bacon. The smashing of the shop windows started about 11 a.m. and within half an hour several shops had had their contents looted by the crowd. One attack was on a shop belonging to a Mrs Sophie Carley who had a butchers shop near to the Attercliffe Church. Her huge plate-glass window was smashed and within seconds the crowd had rushed into the shop and stolen goods. What was even more difficult to understand was the fact that the women and boys did not just attack the shops, but they also broke into the house adjoining it and smashed everything inside that they could lay their hands on. Their work was accompanied by hooting, jeers and laughter as pigs' feet,

Attercliffe rioters in front of shop run by Mrs Carley.

ham, potted meat and various other items came crashing out into the street. It was reported in the *Sheffield Evening Telegraph* that 'a host of women invaded the shop and pulled down all the hanging hams and made away with them'. Some of the women even went upstairs and continued through the bedrooms intent on their work of destruction. Two constables appeared on the scene and attempted to stop the looting, but they were outnumbered by people passing and the traffic which had been forced to stop due to the number of rioters. When other local businesses saw what was happening, they hastily closed their shops and boarded up their windows. Shortly after noon a car full of police officers arrived, but even they seemed helpless as the, by now, large mob then went to Mr Leech, another pork butcher's shop near to Staniforth Road. Once again it was only seconds before his plate-glass window was smashed and the crowd invaded the shop and set to work on the interior. A reporter later stated that Mr Leech told him that he could not explain the reason for the attacks as he was an Englishman born and bred, who had been brought up in Bethnal Road, London. However, he had married a German woman, who had lived in England for thirty-six years. The couple had fled into the yard when the attack began, and when he finally plucked up courage to re-enter his premises, he found an officer taking the names and addresses of several different women who had been caught in his kitchen looting. Not just content to take meat from the shop they had taken gold eye-glasses, two splendid ornaments, a sewing machine, his bank book and his mother's marble clock.

The police officers got into the crowd trying to make them disperse, but the mob just collected a short distance away and went to another shop with a German sounding name. Soon a mounted police officer arrived and he gradually managed to thin the crowd out by weaving his horse in and out of the mob, until finally matters quietened down. The women then gathered outside the shop of Mr Wirth, but they did no more than smash the window, before several police officers arrived to guard the premises, keeping the crowd at a distance. Several women who were waving bunches of black pudding politely requested a press photographer to take a picture of them which he cheerfully obliged. Other shops owned by J. Bullinger and George Hanneman and Sons of Attercliffe were also attacked and looted. Several women had been arrested and taken to Attercliffe Police Station, but were later released as the shopkeepers were too afraid to prosecute the looters.

The following day, before the business of the Sheffield magistrates began, Alderman A.J. Hobson and Alderman A. Balfour made an important statement about the rioting of the previous day, and warned the people of the city that so far the war had been waged on honourable lines by the British Empire. They reminded them that attacks upon civilians were not in accordance with the traditions of our people. One person calling themselves 'Vulcan' wrote to the editor of the *Sheffield Daily*

Women with stolen black puddings posing for reporter.

Telegraph to express her horror at what the women had done. The letter from Hillsborough stated that the women who took part would have been better employed cleaning their houses and the writer hoped that the authorities would make the women replace everything that had been stolen. The letter concluded:

> I am an Englishwoman, first and last, thank God. I never felt more proud to be one than at the present time, but I should not like to take part in wrecking anyone's home, and it is not like our Sheffield women. There are many ways of showing the Germans what we think of them without stealing from them.

Despite this disgraceful rioting episode, it was noticeable that towards the end of the war women were becoming more prominent in the city, to such an extent that the *Sheffield*

Independent commented on the matter. On 25 October 1917 the paper reported that local women now had a voice and they were not afraid to speak articulately at the Labour Congress, the Co-operative Conference and the council meetings of the NUWW. The reporter stated that 'some of these views were distinctly advanced, and yet just three years ago their holders would have been gasped at for their temerity in voicing them in public'. A week later there was to be a conference at the Montgomery Hall where women's organisations were gathering together to consider their new responsibilities and in particular equal pay for equal work. By the end of the year the NUWW was demanding that Sheffield women must now unite to demand the vote in order to make effective changes. The speaker Mrs Hudson Lyall stated that the vote was a sacred trust, and must be used on local bodies where women could inspire greater progress than had been made so far. She said that there was still prejudice against women on these bodies, but she hoped that it was rapidly disappearing. The following year the NUWW changed its name to the National Council of Women of Great Britain (NCW).

Finally on 11 November 1918 the end of the war was announced, and the *Sheffield Daily Telegraph* reported the jubilation in the streets of the city as people celebrated the end of the war. Headlines described their joy such as 'Sheffield Still Soberly Jubilant'. Incredibly for a city where drinking had become a problem only a few years previously, there were few reports of drunkenness as workers abandoned their posts and headed for the moors. Munitions women were among many others who, escaping from the heat and din of the steelworks, were enjoying the keen bracing air. Meanwhile it was also reported that throngs of people, men as well as women, wandered around the streets in triumph. In January 1919 the same newspaper praised in particular the work undertaken by women during the duration of the Great War. It stated that looking over the field of national activity, it was almost impossible to point a finger to where the women of Sheffield had not made their influence felt. The reporter specifically praised the conductresses, women working on the railway, postal workers, Clerks at the Town Hall, and on gas inspection work. He stated that they had undertaken such tasks 'without any of the nervousness erroneously associated with their sex'. He continued that praise should also be reflected on the doctors and police officers who had rendered such splendid service to the city, but added that although at that time there were no women lawyers 'undoubtedly their influence will be felt in the Sheffield of the future'. Finally he remarked on the way in which ordinary Sheffield women, unable to commit to more important roles had also contributed. He concluded:

> There has been that body of women who have given ungrudging service in raising funds for the various war charities by way of flag days, special concerts, and the dozen and one ways in which money is secured for charitable objects. Sheffield can certainly point with pride to the record of its women during the Great War.

The actuality of Sheffield women working at roles formerly undertaken only by men had given them a confidence that had not been present before the war. Although it was naturally understood by society that women would go back to their place in the home once they were no longer needed, for some there was no going back. Sheffield women had experienced a greater freedom, not only with the pay in their pockets, but also by becoming a valuable asset to the country. On 6 February 1918 the Representation of the People Act was finally passed through Parliament, allowing all men over 21 and women over 30 the right to vote. The ex-suffragettes were only partly jubilant due to the limitations of the Act and the inequalities within it. Women over 30 could only vote providing they or their husbands met the property qualifications, whereas for male voters there were no property limitations. It had also been suggested that women were being rewarded with the vote for their role in the Great War, with a patronising pat on the back for all their hard work. In fact most women who had served in the war were too young or too poor to vote and were not rewarded in any way for another ten years.

CHAPTER EIGHT

The Interwar Years

Now that certain women of Sheffield had the vote, it was soon predicted that it would undoubtedly increase the number of votes in the local elections. The *Sheffield Daily Telegraph* for 22 February 1918 estimated that in Sheffield alone the numbers of voters had increased from 61,663 to approximately 165,000. Despite the fact that the vote excluded many local women, the same newspaper reminded those that were newly enfranchised: 'You did not fail when called upon to help your country to win the war. There were 5,000 women engaged in one munitions factory alone in the city, the majority from Sheffield and its surrounding districts.'

But there followed some very patronising information as to exactly how these women, some of whom had previously worked with complicated machines and lathes during the war, should now actually use that vote. It described in great detail how to mark the paper with a cross, fold it and deposit it in the box, as it would to a two-year-old child. Just to make sure the message got across, the paper repeated it again the following Saturday, adding that if a woman felt nervous then she should take a friend with her, adding unnecessarily that the friend would not be allowed into the 'box like compartment'.

Although a great proportion of politicians now hoped that women would go back to their passive and subservient role they had held before the war, it would seem that nothing could reverse the freedom they had experienced. The same newspaper put it succinctly a week later describing a despondent girl, one of hundreds who was now:

> Back again at flowers, dusting the drawing room - with a big heart ache. Her day is spent secretly repining. She has the ability to work, but is not allowed to. She craves for independence - but it is not fashionable; and she pines for the good old days of the war.

Many of those who had been employed during the war found that there was no way back now that many of their temporary jobs had been given to disabled ex-servicemen. The Sheffield Employment Exchange looked at ways of employing these women in traditionally domestic skills, which it claimed would give them more employment opportunities. Premises on Bailey Street, Sheffield were made available as a Domestic Centre in November 1919 where women were to be taught dressmaking. The Exchange claimed that same month, that fifty-eight girls had already started their training, using the wartime habit of not only creating new items from pretty materials but also recycling older garments. A demonstration of their work took place a couple of months later in January 1920 where beautifully sewed creations in silk and crepe-de-chine were on show. There was also a selection of skirts and dresses which had been renovated from old coats. The old hang-up from pre-war days of a girl needing to have a good character was still seen as important. The *Sheffield Independent* of 21 January proudly noted that at the end of her training 'each girl had earned for herself a good character from her teachers for her industry and attention to duty'. One of the organisers, Mr James Graham proudly told a reporter that Sheffield had been the first place in the country to develop such schemes, but now another thousand women were also being trained in other areas of Yorkshire. Mr Graham said that the following week the newly-trained girls will be ready to start work, and that some of them will be employed at the workrooms on Bailey Street. Others will go out by the day to ladies' houses to undertake the family sewing, or they might work from their own homes. He stated that 'anybody who requires the services of a little dressmaker should apply to Miss Sheard at the Women's Employment Exchange, East Parade, Sheffield, where she can make a careful selection of the appropriate seamstress according to the need'.

Other Sheffield women were encouraged to go back to the kinds of domestic services they had undertaken before the war. Indeed it appeared to be the chief demand in Sheffield in February 1920, where it was said that the demand for girls to live in as domestic servants was greater than the supply of women available. Nevertheless many women were not interested in going back to work in a role they saw as mere skivvies, after the freedom they had experienced over the last four years. Another Domestic College in Leopold Street was also training local women in March 1920 who had served with the forces as WAAFs during the war, to do cookery courses. It was said that although many of them had not cooked a potato before the hostilities, now they could be trained as professional cooks. The qualifications they then earned would guarantee them competence to find employment as cooks or as cook/ housekeepers in domestic service. Once again Miss Sheard awaited applications from employers requiring such qualified workers. In May 1920 the Rev. W.P. Wright the vicar of St Silas, Sheffield stoutly championed the role of the domestic servant. At the Annual General Meeting of the Sheffield Servants Home he told the audience that domestic service:

> was one of the most ancient, and surely one of the most honourable calling. Unfortunately in these days there was a sort of stigma upon domestic service, and there were cases where those who entered domestic service were not treated as they should be. Domestic service now-a-days was one of the last occupations to which a woman would turn.

Even women's columns of the local newspapers joined in the drive to encourage women back into their previously domestic roles. Throughout the 1920s the *Sheffield Telegraph* published a column which was stated to be written especially for women called the 'Woman's World' which showed the latest fashions. Despite its contents, which were light in nature consisting mainly of cookery tips, and descriptions of local weddings, there was a presumption that the reporter was probably male. This is revealed in the didactic nature instructing Sheffield women on how they should or should not behave, and was a typical male perspective of the period. The column warned of the dangers for women in the 'equal-pay-for-equal-work' movement that was sweeping across local women's groups. On 28 September 1920 the columnist emphasised how this was not conducive to the physical well-being of the woman in the labour market of the period. The reporter claimed that:

> in order to obtain the same wages as men, women often have to work at excessive pressure, for unduly long hours as in the days of sweated labour to achieve the same as men. Those unaccustomed to such long hours may lose her head in her anxiety 'to make

A Smart Hat for this Season's Wear.

Typical fashion picture in 'Woman's World' column.

hay while the sun shines' thereby taxing her strength both physically and mentally to a dangerous degree.

The unnamed writer of the article listed only by the initials 'A.C.', goes on to suggest that by over-production the woman's work will inevitably deteriorate. So it is unsurprising then that in the March 1921 edition the author states with some authority that many 'women were not ready for the franchise when they got it'. Concluding that 'they have never known and do not care anything about the problems of life' which the writer blamed on 'fundamental lack of intelligence and sympathy'. I suspect that any of the suffragettes that still lived in the city would be wringing their hands in despair at this writer's attitude.

In the first few months of 1921 the columnist also questions whether women are actually capable of becoming engineers, despite the fact that many local women had been trained in engineering during the war. Later that same year, as if to prove the writer wrong, one of the first of these Sheffield women to get her engineering degree was Miss Alice Katherine Osbourne who received her diploma from the Vice Chancellor of the University of Sheffield in July 1921. It was noted that her achievement had been made, despite the fact that all the other recipients of the engineering degrees were male. The following month the writer returns to the theme of whether women were capable of becoming engineers, stating:

> Engineering in its widest sense needs the mechanically constructive brain, and for big undertakings and invention, a length of vision and capacity to grasp complex things that is rarely included in the make-up of women. Women were not made for the sterner things of life, and engineering is one of the sternest.

Despite the columnist's patronising tone it was evident that Sheffield women were now taking full advantage of a university education. That very same month there were nineteen other successful women qualifying for a Master in Arts, twenty-two gaining Batchelor of Arts degrees and fifteen women gaining a diploma in education at the same award ceremony.

Another monumental struggle which the women of Sheffield had to fight long and hard for, was for the city to have women police officers. In fact the situation was to prove almost as big a battle as the suffragettes had found when they first started talking about female equality. To break down the bastion of male dominated status would take years to achieve. Initially the idea was soundly opposed by the all-male Watch Committee, and it was only when women were elected as justices of the peace and thanks to the campaigning of other female groups, such as the NCW, were they successful. The first women patrols had left the people of Sheffield with a deep understanding of how essential women could be in the police force, particularly in dealing with other women and children. Because of these patrols, for probably the first time, the legal authorities of Sheffield started to consider employing a woman police officer.

The first WPC ever to serve in the whole of Britain who had the powers of arrest, had been a woman called Mrs Edith Smith who had been appointed to the Grantham Police Force in August 1915. The following year on 23 November 1916 she came to Sheffield to give a talk to the annual meeting of the NUWW on her roles and responsibilities. She told her audience that she investigated all the cases which involved women and children, and acted as a probation officer for girls in court. Mrs Smith told them that she loved her job and the ceremony of 'swearing in' had left her with a deep sense of awe and tremendous importance, which she still retained. Interestingly at the same time, the Home Office were warning that women could not be sworn in as police officers, as they were 'not proper persons' because at that time they could not vote in parliamentary elections or serve on juries. However, Mrs Smith said that she was treated with the greatest respect by other members of the public, and had easily quelled violent disturbances with little difficulty.

The conflict in Sheffield had begun in August 1917 when someone who signed themselves 'NOT A WOMAN HATER' wrote to the editor of the *Sheffield Independent* asking 'is it not time for women police officers to be introduced in the city?' The writer claimed:

> As one walks about the streets, the flappers with the short skirts, pencilled eyes and hair covered ears, who parade or stand in groups obstructing traffic in our principal streets are a public nuisance. Let the Watch Committee appoint women police at once.

The Chief Constable of Sheffield, Major Hall-Dalwood actually agreed with this view and stated that he would be quite happy to employ women officers, providing they were adequately supervised. He claimed to be quite in favour of women police so long as they were selected from the 'right sort of women' and were thoroughly trained. However, the question of the acceptance of WPCs in Sheffield was not his to appoint, as that responsibility lay with the Sheffield Watch Committee and they were opposed to women acting in any official capacity. It was generally thought that it was not fitting for women to deal with drunken men and they were deemed to be incapable of controlling crowds. Despite this, the NUWW persisted in demanding female officers, and so finally on 8 December 1917 the Sheffield Watch Committee recommended that for a trial period two female constables might be appointed. Their wages were to be two guineas a week (£2.2s) although it is worth recording that male officers earned 70s a week at that time (£3.10s). The women were also to have a uniform allowance of 7s 6d a week, which, it was suggested, would barely keep them in shoe repairs. The Watch Committee's reluctance to appoint the women was confirmed when they held their meeting three days later on 11 December 1917, when members complained that it was difficult to specify what work could be allocated to the female officers; but there was some delay in between the recommendation that the officers be appointed, and putting it into action.

Consequently, it was not until March 1918 that the first WPC was finally appointed in Sheffield. She was Miss Mary E. Winn and she was joined by a Miss Lovell who was appointed two months later. It had been decided that their duties were to patrol the streets day and night, to work with children and to be of value in the police courts, in other words they were to replicate the way in which the women's patrols had operated during the war. There is little evidence of how welcome the two women were made in Sheffield, although it was a given that they would not prove popular with the Watch Committee. Sadly they were also criticised by people of Sheffield too. The following October these women were described as being 'grim, gaunt women in blue, with flat brimmed hats'.

It is not known when Miss Winn resigned, but by 14 December 1921 the Sheffield Town Council meeting commented on the fact that the remaining officer, Miss Lovell had now also resigned, and that once again there would be no female police officers employed in the city police force. When the question was asked about recruiting some more, the Watch Committee were once more reluctant. Alderman Cattell, the chair of the Watch Committee, explained that the project had been given an extended trial, but said that they were not in favour of engaging any more women in the city. Despite this, he was overruled when both Alderman Marsh and Councillor Mrs Wilkinson not only asked for an increase in the number of women police in Sheffield, but also requested that better use be made of their services. The following month it was announced that the matter was to be referred to a sub-committee for their consideration. Despite this, the Geddes Report of 1922, from a committee asked to look into government expenditure, described the work of the metropolitan WPCs as 'negligible' and recommended their disbandment. The former NUWW, which was now known as the National Council of Women (NCW), formed a deputation to the Home Secretary, Edward Shortt but it was wasted effort as he stated that 'the work of the women officers could not possibly be described as police work, and that it was more in the nature of welfare work'.

The Sex Disqualification (Removal) Act was brought in by December 1919, but its remit was very broad and it took years to enforce. Meanwhile the NCW was still urging that more female officers be appointed for the city. Consequently it was not until May 1923 that the Sheffield Watch Committee were forced to reluctantly employ just one female officer with limited powers. When the Government Departmental Committee report regarding the employment of WPCs in England and Wales was published in August 1924, it was in favour. However, it stated that although the efficiency of the police force had been 'improved by the employment of policewomen' the report stipulated that they should be employed from all grades of educated women and not 'vinegary spinsters or blighted middle aged fanatics'. The Sheffield Watch Committee were still reluctant and said that they did not deem it necessary at that time to appoint any more WPCs. A deputation of five Sheffield women magistrates waited on the Watch Committee on 5 February 1925, to ask what steps it was proposing to take regarding carrying out the recommendations of the Home Office to employ more female officers. The local newspaper commented that between late autumn of 1913 and spring of 1924, a total of sixteen Sheffield charity committees had sent resolutions to the Watch Committee urging the employment of more WPCs. A member of the Watch Committee spoke to a reporter and stated that at that time the main crimes in Sheffield were gang rowdyism, burglaries, shop breaking and street betting. He claimed that policewomen would not be of any use in such cases. Magistrate, Mrs Longden, disagreed and said that in her experience WPCs were urgently needed in the city. Alderman Cattell, the chair of the Watch Committee argued that they needed about 300 more male officers to be appointed, rather than just a few women. The argument reached its zenith in May 1925 when the City Council passed a resolution that four more female police officers were to be employed, but the resolution was rejected by the Watch Committee as being unnecessary. In retaliation the City Council refused to pass the minutes of the Watch Committee. Alderman Marsh complained that minutes were brought before the council to approve them, not to express an opinion and they had no power to vary any of the decisions made by another committee.

Mrs Longden asked if they could appeal straight to the Home Office to over-rule the decision of the Watch Committee.

Meanwhile, the NCW and other women's organisations continued to agitate for more female officers, and as a result it was finally announced in October 1925 that two new policewomen were coming to Sheffield the following week. Their credentials were impeccable as both women were very experienced in conflict having been with the Army of Occupation in the Rhine Valley and both had served as nurses. A deputation from women's organisations in December of the same year, urged support for a bill in the Commons which demanded that local Watch Committees should be compelled to appoint WPCs. Once again the Sheffield Watch Committee refused, stating that instead women should use their votes to elect councillors who were sympathetic to the appointment of female police officers. But the value of having a woman on the police force was outlined by a report from the committee on Offences against Young Persons. The report agreed that properly trained women should take the statements of young girls in sensitive cases, or at the very least be in attendance whilst a male officer takes the statement. It also recommended that a female doctor should be in attendance for any medical examination of women or girls in similar cases. It is difficult to know exactly how the Sheffield WPCs were utilized, although the local newspapers found at least one case where they had been found to be useful. Three of the policewomen of Sheffield had been used in a fortune-telling case which was discovered in January 1926. They had been sent out to a house in Chatham Street, Sheffield in plain clothes to present themselves as customers to a woman called Mary Simpson. Interestingly the fortune-teller was right in one prediction where she told them that they 'were much among officers' but added that they were all going to have happy marriages and plenty of money. The officers who were named as Miss Mary Morris, Miss Mary Wynne and Miss Watson gave evidence that they had kept watch on a shop from where Mrs Simpson operated, and saw many women going in and out. As customers they would stay for quite a while, but always left

CAPTAIN P. J. SILLITOE.

Captain P.J. Sillitoe who welcomed the introduction of WPCs to Sheffield.

the shop without carrying any bundles of shopping. Mrs Simpson's defence was that, although she did not deny telling fortunes she had been pestered by the disguised policewomen into telling their fortune, claiming that it was them who persuaded her to commit the offence. She was found guilty and fined.

In May 1927 it was reported that the Chief Constable of Sheffield, Captain P.J. Sillitoe had reported very favourably on the work of the city's policewomen. He had written an article for the first issue of a publication entitled *The Policewoman's Review* where he wrote:

I am a firm believer in the usefulness of, and necessity for, women police [...] We have at the present time, only three policewomen on our strength, but they are fully sworn in, and the general knowledge of their status and powers give them added authority and prestige in dealing with the public.

He outlined their duties which did not just involve street and park patrols, but also investigations for the Home Office and Ministry of Pensions, escorting female prisoners, accompanying male detectives when arresting women, plain-clothes work, searching houses, taking statements from women, girls and children in cases of indecency and attending court. He concluded by saying that 'I believe in women police, given the right type of highly educated women.' By October of 1928 it was announced that three more policewomen were to be added to the force, due to the fact that sexual crime in Sheffield was on the increase. The women were to be paid 60*s* a week on appointment, which would be gradually increased as they became more experienced. There is little doubt that the victory that Sheffield women felt on the appointment of these WPCs was down to the efforts of the NCW and other women's organisations, despite much condemnation by higher officials. Major General Sir Wyndham Childs, Assistant Commissioner of the Metropolitan Police himself, during an enquiry in October 1928, stated that some female officers were 'No use to the CID except in cases of watching the passing of cocaine or in the case of clairvoyants. [...] They were not of sufficient use to the CID to warrant putting them on staff.'

One women who certainly loved her job was Sergeant Mary Morris who told a reporter in October of 1930 that of the six women police officers now operating in the city, they all

Sheffield policewoman in uniform.

radiated the most cheerful outlook in their work. Nevertheless the hostility towards WPCs still continued. So when it was proposed that two more women, Gwendolyn M. Edgely and Norah P. Gray were to be appointed in February 1932, their appointment caused a storm at the City Council meeting held on 3 February. It was reported that two council members 'were at a loss to understand what women police do throughout the day'. Councillor Geoffrey Chambers and Councillor H. Morris declared that they seem to spend their time in the police courts every morning, but could not understand what else they did. Both offered the opinion that they hoped that no new female officers would be appointed. Councillor Mrs Ada Moore took exception to her colleagues attempting, as she put it, 'to get the women dismissed' and reminded them that the WPC's duties were not just to shine in the police court, but were proving to be very efficient behind the scenes. Gradually women police officers proved their worth in Sheffield as they undertook the same roles and responsibilities as male officers, but I suspect it would be a long time before the initial hostility disappeared altogether.

The interwar years also saw political history made in Sheffield on 10 November 1919 where it was noted that for the very first time in the city's history, a woman had spoken in council as member of the Maternity and Child Welfare committee. Councillor Mrs Gertrude Wilkinson was well-known as an organiser for the General Worker's Union and Vice President of the Labour Party. She stated that she had great pleasure in supporting the election of the newest Lord Mayor of Sheffield, Mr Samuel Roberts and praised his services to the health of the city, in particular his great efforts to ensure a pure milk supply. Much later the *Sheffield Independent* of 28 May 1927, when discussing Mrs Wilkinson, conceded that 'her career was a striking justification for the extension of the franchise to women'. Despite this, at that time it was noted that there were no elected female members on the City Council. Yet as far back as September 1918, questions were being asked as to why there were not more elected women. The *Sheffield Independent* printed an article that month stating that 'now women have the parliamentary vote, isn't it time they set about altering the character of the City Council?' The article stated that 'most of the members were elected back in the dark ages of feminine suppression, adding that whilst it was true that:

> the Distress Committee, the Education Committee and committees dealing with mental defectives, Old Age Pension, Food Control and the King Edward Hospital for Crippled Children have women members, they are co-opted and not elected by the citizens. Consequently whilst having influence such as members, they have no power and are not expected to seek any.

The article continued to point out 'the cleansing of the streets was as much women's concerns as the men's? But it was not until 1 November 1920 that Sheffield saw an elected councillor for the Attercliffe Ward, when Mrs Eleanor Barton won the seat by a majority of 906 votes. She came from a family that had long been active in the Labour movement and was the wife of Alfred Barton, who himself was reported to be 'an active anarchist'. Nevertheless it was said that his wife was 'seen to be more dangerous than her husband'. In her election poster she claimed to be devoting herself to bettering the position of local women promising to be 'The True Friend of Women and Children'. Mrs Barton was therefore delighted to be Sheffield's first woman elected alongside fifteen other male councillors. Her election had been a popular victory, to the point where her jubilant supporters carried her shoulder-high from the Vestry Hall to the Baths Corner in Sheffield. Despite her own enthusiasm, it was reported that she looked very relieved as she was placed once more on her feet. Little research has been undertaken on the reception which these pioneer women received from the previously all-male town and city councils. Any woman might have found it very difficult to get beyond the powerful aldermanic bench, and no doubt it would have taken quite a while to understand the proceedings of the town council and its complexities. How much help they received from their new colleagues is open to question, but these women were certainly the pioneers of women councillors today.

But in Sheffield it was not until 1928 (seventy-seven years after the formation of the SWPA in 1851) that the efforts of the suffragists and suffragettes finally paid off when the Amendment to the Representation of the People Act was passed. Now everyone over the age of 21, men and women, was finally given the power to vote. But perhaps the greatest achievement for Sheffield women took place on 5 August 1936 when it was announced that a woman, Mrs Ann Eliza Longden,

DAILY INDEPENDENT PHOTOGRAPH
Miss Ethel Mannin (left) at the opening of Book Week at Sheffield Central Library yesterday. The Lord Mayor (Mrs. Longden) presided and was accompanied by the Lady Mayoress (Miss Longden).

Mrs Longden as Sheffield Lord Mayor and her daughter as Lady Mayoress.

was to be nominated as Sheffield's first female Lord Mayor. Her daughter Mary aged 28, would serve as one of the youngest Lady Mayoress' in the country. Mrs Longden, who had been a representative of Hillsborough Ward since 1922, had long been involved in the establishment of Sheffield's Maternity and Child Welfare clinics. Once the nomination had been announced however, the main topic of conversation in the city was how, as a woman, Mrs Longden would be dealt with by the Master Cutler at the next Cutler's Feast. Traditionally this exclusively all-male organisation held an annual ceremony which had been in existence for 300 years in the city, and to which was invited only the most prominent men of the town. The Feast had always been closed to all women who were confined to the Ladies Gallery or the Lady Cutlers drawing room, whilst the men were royally entertained. When Mrs Longden was informed of her election by a reporter from the *Sheffield Independent*, he asked her 'will you be content to sit in the Ladies Gallery?' to which she simply replied 'Ah' with a laugh. There was one concession that Mrs Longden did make to her historic role, which was to order new robes, as she told the reporter that the old ones had been worn since the time when the Duke of Norfolk was the Lord Mayor in 1895. Her new robe was described as weighing much lighter in scarlet-corded silk, faced with black velvet and brown fur. Mrs Longden had also ordered two smaller tri-corn hats, one for ceremonial occasions and the other for informal outdoor occasions made in the same design with black feathers fringing the brim, and a gold-braided tab in the front.

On Monday, 9 November 1936, Mrs Longden was officially sworn in as Lord Mayor of Sheffield, as she stood to attention to receive the gold chain of office, dwarfed by the back of the Lord Mayor's chair. That same afternoon she attended her first council meeting in that capacity as she told the assembled council: 'The only qualifications I have for this position are a high sense of duty, a bit of business ability, a certain amount of common sense and a strong earnest desire to serve my fellow men and women.'

She concluded that it was not just an honour for herself but 'it is a great honour for all the women of Sheffield'. Among one of her first duties, she was to attend the civic procession for the Armistice celebrations in Sheffield in her mayoral robes. Mrs Longden also made more history with another first, when she became the first woman Lord Mayor to attend the Coronation of George VI and Elizabeth Bowes-Lyon, on 12 May 1937. She also broke another long-held taboo when attending in her official capacity at the Judges Banquet in Leeds, in her ceremonial robes. On that occasion she stated that she had been so nervous, that the only thought that re-assured her was that at the later Cutlers Feast in Sheffield, at least she would know most of the people there. When the Feast was duly held on 1 November 1937 as Mrs Longden took her place in the banqueting hall, it was reported that she was conspicuously the only female in a room of men. A reporter described the occasion as 'barriers of tradition fell graciously away' as Mrs Longden took her place between the Bishop of Sheffield and Mr Leslie Burgin, the Minister for Transport. A reporter could not help making the reference to the only other woman who had tried to crash the Feast, when Miss Adela Pankhurst tried unsuccessfully to gain entry to the Hall dressed as a kitchen maid in November 1908. Despite Mrs Longden's enthusiasm, when she finally relinquished her role after a year she stated that she would not have wanted to serve another year as Lord Mayor of Sheffield.

It was not until 1949 that a second women, Grace Tebbutt, was elected into the same position. She had grown up in Attercliffe and had been elected onto the council in 1929, just ten years after women had been given the vote. Grace Tebbutt was also a magistrate, and during the time that she served on the council she had taken a great interest in unmarried mothers and children. This second person to take on the most prestigious role in the history of the city was made a Dame of the British Empire in 1966 and died in 1983. Another prominent Sheffield women was Patricia Sheard who was elected onto the council in 1945 and served until 1984. She too was to become another Lord Mayor of Sheffield, in 1968.

Throughout the interwar years Sheffield women had proved that they could build on the experiences that they had gained through the First World War. They quickly learned skills which gave them confidence, proving both to themselves and the rest of the world that they were the equal of men. Women had taken on roles which could only have been dreamt of around fifty years earlier, and had smashed forever the ideology of the separate spheres. Women like Mary Anne Rawson and Anne Knight could not have visualised that a Sheffield woman would have spoken in front of male members of the town council, serve on the City Council or indeed have been elected Lord Mayor. Women had indeed come a long way, but by July 1939 the success of Sheffield women and the great strides made by them were about to be challenged once more, as preparations for the Second World War began.

CHAPTER NINE

Women of Steel

Once again when war was declared on 3 September 1939, the people of Sheffield braced themselves for the struggle ahead. Local women prepared to meet the war with bravery and fortitude, as one housewife quite honestly told a reporter from the *Sheffield Independent* a week later, 'frankly I am frightened to death, but we must hope for the best, whilst providing for the worst'. Almost immediately shoppers found that there was a shortage of torches and batteries as housewives tried to stock up on these kinds of emergency goods which would be essential in the days ahead. For the second time in twenty-five years the many steelworks and workshops of the city were turned towards making armaments. The city knew that it would become a prime target, as for the first eighteen months of the war the Vickers works was the only place in the country that had a drop hammer capable of forging crankshafts for the Spitfires of the RAF. They also made bullet-proof plates to protect the planes and pilots during battle and this would make the city a high-priority target for German bombs. When the announcement was made that Britain was at war with Germany, many Sheffield people were still in church. For a while the only ones visible in the streets were those employed at filling sandbags, but then as common sense took over, people rejoined their normal duties of visiting friends and taking a stroll around the Peace Gardens.

Almost as soon as the war was announced local women were prominent in the news, but it was not so much in their

The Peace Gardens as they look today.

A SOLDIER'S FAMILY OF SOLDIERS.

Sergt. John Wrigley, of the R.A.M.C., and engaged at the 3rd Northern General Hospital, has five soldier sons. Our pictures are of the soldier father, the five sons, and the proud mother.

ANOTHER SHEFFIELD GROUP OF SOLDIER SONS.

Mr. and Mrs. ? Kaell, who resue at 55, Coningsby road, have given five sons to the Army. They are, from left to right, Joseph. Frederick, Richard, killed at the Dardanelles; Harry, and Wilfred. We also give pictures of the father and mother.

Proud Sheffield mothers with multiple sons fighting in the Second World War.

own right, but as those who had husbands and multiple sons fighting in the war. These women who remained at home were the primary recipients of the news that their loved ones had been injured or killed. Every day the local newspapers listed the names of the city men who had died, or who had been injured in the fighting. Thankfully, some women were luckier in that they received news that their relative had not died, but had been taken prisoner of war and would, hopefully, return home at the end of the hostilities. Such a person was Miss Jessie Horton of Bramall Lane, Sheffield in August 1940 who was told that Private Walter Derbyshire aged 22, to whom she was engaged, had been reported as missing on 11 July. Other news about a missing soldier came at the same time, just after his wife, Mrs F. Stone of Holme Lane, Sheffield had given birth to twins, a boy and a girl. Private Stone had been reported missing on 12 July and had last been heard of in Abbeville, France. Both men were now reported to have been taken prisoner. However, occasionally there was better news such as that received on the last day of August 1940 when Miss Edna Mokes of Alnwick Road, Sheffield actually received a letter from her fiancé, Driver J.P. Dewhurst who had been presumed dead. He wrote: 'I have been wounded and am now a prisoner of war. I am getting along fine and am getting about again. Give my love to all at home and tell them I am always thinking about them.'

Initially, as in the First World War, women were once more relegated to the domestic tasks of sewing and knitting garments for the men fighting at the front. By January 1940 these knitting groups were being organised by the Mistress Cutler, Mrs Ashley S. Ward. She told a reporter that there were, at that time, 217 knitting work parties totalling 1,900 women throughout the city. A new movement had just begun for women to knit garments which were purely for the Royal Navy. They met every Friday in the lounge of the Regent Cinema, Barkers Pool for sharing knitting and coffee. Other women from the Christian Temperance Association chose to serve cheap meals to members of the armed forces at the Fleur De Lis cafe, Fargate, Sheffield. There, service men home on leave could buy subsidised meals of beans on toast with tea for sixpence, or bread and dripping for a halfpenny. Games and writing equipment were available for them to write home and posters on the walls advised them to 'Remember the Folks at Home' and 'Be the Man your Mother thinks you are'.

Past experience showed that women could immediately replace the regular postmen as the men were called up. As early as Christmas 1939 it was announced that around 500 were needed and the Sheffield Postmaster immediately found himself inundated with applicants. Once again assurances were sought that women engaging in 'men's work' would automatically step down at the end of the war when they returned from the front line. Those men who had formerly been employed in such jobs expressed some concerns because as the women were lower paid, the men thought that they would have to work at a reduced wage when they returned home. By May 1940 it was announced that bus and tram conductresses were again needed although, because of shift work, at first only single women were required. In June 1940 the first batch of twelve were being trained, and it was reported that they were to have a much smarter uniform than that worn by their mothers twenty-five years previously. In February 1941 girl porters were being employed at the railway station at Sheffield. Although they had no uniforms at that time, they wore a peaked hat with the word 'porter' picked out in brightly-polished metal letters. Supervisor, Mrs E. Machin of Dryden Road, Parsons Cross, Sheffield, soon organised the rest of their regular uniforms, and in May 1941 she told a reporter that twelve girls had already been fitted with them the day before. Apart from the hat, they now had dark-blue jacket and a blouse to match. Mrs Machin explained that their duties included the carrying of luggage, although she added that if the bags were too heavy men were always glad to help the girls out. Four other women were employed as railway-carriage cleaners and like the porters they shared any tips they received.

Barrage balloons played a large part in the Second World War in Sheffield, in order to protect the city and its output of steel production. Squadrons of reservists had formed three groups before the war who undertook training at weekends, and were called No 16 Balloon Centre based at Lightwood, later renamed RAF Norton. During the war the siting of the balloons over the city gave a great sense of security and protection, which was deemed essential for the people's morale. These balloons were also vital for protection against low-flying aircraft, forcing them to fly at a much higher altitude and into the range of anti-aircraft guns. Although many technical modifications had taken place in balloon handling, and much of the hard manual work had been mechanised, it was initially not seen as a job that women could do.

In June 1939 it was decided by the RAF that Sheffield would have a Women's Auxiliary Air Force (WAAF) unit and that some of them would be allocated to RAF Norton. When it was suggested, early in 1941, that these women might be used to deal with the barrage balloons there was a public outcry. The matter had been brought to the attention of the public by a question asked in the House of Commons in May 1941 suggesting that women could manipulate the barrage balloons and release the men for more important and heavy work. Once again it was stated that women were not strong enough for the job. The *Star* dated 12 May 1941 reported reasons why the women would be unsuitable:

> Most of the balloon sites are in exposed places, living conditions are very rough, and to handle a balloon in a breeze is heavy work even for a physically fit man. An unfit man would be entirely incapable of doing the work.

Nevertheless women were recruited and it was finally agreed that the WAAFs of RAF Norton would be utilized to handle the balloons as an experiment for the rest of Britain. They were told that the whole manning policy of the Balloon Command depended on their success. On average the balloons were about 6,000 feet high in the air and fairly unwieldy to handle, nevertheless these women did a spectacular job. The original teams were made up of women who were already used to working in the balloon repair shops at various centres around the city. They undertook a rigorous and lengthy training at Cardington, where the first British airships had been stationed. As a result in 1942 RAF Norton was selected to be the leading centre for the training of WAAF airwomen from all over the country in barrage balloon duties. Some 1,000 WAAF officers, NCOs and airwomen came to Sheffield to learn how to work the balloons. Inevitably there was much secrecy around the work of the WAAF and the barrage balloons. The women did a great job and it was only as the war neared its end, and the need for inland barrages ceased, that the balloon protection of Sheffield ceased.

As the war progressed Sheffield women took on much heavier jobs, as they had before in the Great War. In February 1942 it was announced that women were now working as bridge painters, plate laying and undertaking general track maintenance. These boiler-suited women were described as 'tough, hardworking with steady nerves who worked in all weathers. They sometimes worked forty to fifty feet in the air, over tracks and tidal rivers, often balanced on narrow planks, singing as they worked'. Some were mothers with babies as young as five and seven months, who they had left with neighbours. Most of them had never worked before, and were now employed as labourers. They started at 7.30 a.m. and worked until 5 p.m. with only an hour's break for dinner. For a forty-seven-hour week they earned just 71s 6d (£3.11s) which it was claimed was equivalent to what it had been for male labourers before the war. Because of the heavy work, all the women were allowed supplementary cheese and milk rations. Other women preferred to work in canning factories engaged in the task of conserving the nation's food supplies. When a reporter from the *Sheffield Independent* arrived at Batchelor's Peas Ltd., Wadsley Bridge, Sheffield, he found 600 girls working at top speed, packing millions of tins full of strawberries, gooseberries, cherries and plums. He reported that where previously the firm would have used imported fruit, they were now having to rely on local home-grown crops. The scheme had been so successful that the girls were working day and night to fulfil their orders.

Through the use of propaganda the role of being only 'a housewife' was now made a patriotic duty, as these women were seen as heroines where conservation of food was concerned and something that everyone was encouraged to do. From the outset of the war they were advised not to panic buy, as they would be acting against the national interest. A story was circulated in the city at the time which illustrated the unpatriotic nature of stockpiling. It concerned a local shopkeeper who was asked for a large number of tinned goods, and he asked his female customer if she thought her actions were 'decent'. The woman thought about it for a moment and after some reflection reduced the size of her order. The war had barely started before housewives were praised for the frugality of the meals they served their families. One woman, Mrs J. Rollins of Shiregreen, Sheffield was the subject of an article on 'thrift in the kitchen' as early as December 1939. It was reported that after queuing for hours she managed to get a marrow bone for 6d, out of which she made a stew that the family had for dinner, 1lb of potted meat and ½lb of cooking fat. The article stated that because their men are doing 'a real job of work' at the moment, women had to be more adaptable. One way in which they could do this was by being careful with the family's meals. Another woman, Mrs Shepherd, told the same reporter that she could make an attractive meal out of fried onions, potatoes and gravy. Mrs Edward Long of Broad Lane, Sheffield also carefully planned her wartime menus for her husband and two sons. She stated heroically that she didn't require bacon in a morning and so gave her ration to her menfolk. Even the Lady Mayoress, Mrs Luther Milner added her way of providing good wholesome food in January 1941 when she described a meatless dinner she had provided for her husband. She had made fish cakes using a tin of salmon and fresh white herrings, mixed with boiled potatoes, turnips and brown gravy. Her efforts were praised to be as patriotic as the men serving at the front, as she described how she did all her own baking, including bread, and made her own jam, pickles and bottled fruit. Proud Sheffield housewives showed the Princess Royal, on a visit to Sheffield, how adaptable they had become in August of 1942. Following lessons learned from the devastation of the blitz of Sheffield in December 1940, they prepared a meal which was cooked and eaten in the street. The meal consisted of vegetable stew, new potatoes and steamed chocolate pudding, which had been made in open-air ovens made of bricks, mud and debris. It was reported that it took just half a bucket of coal to cook meals for fifty people.

For entertainment most young women of Sheffield went to the cinema in December 1939 where they could see the latest films *Andy Hardy Gets Spring Fever* starring Mickey Rooney at the Regent, or *Confessions of a Nazi Spy* at the Central Cinema. One of the most controversial requests from the people of Sheffield, to open cinemas during the day and particularly at weekends, was consistently turned down by the Sheffield Watch Committee. The local cinemas were the subject of an experiment in August 1949 when a plan to show free documentary Ministry of Information films was proposed. Lasting anything from five to twenty minutes, the films were to focus on such subjects as Britain's fighting forces, home defence, Britain's sea power, the Empire, health and fitness, or salvage and food; but there is little evidence as to whether these were successful or not. The

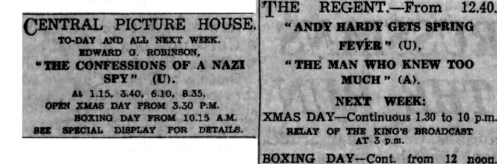

Advert for films showing in Sheffield in December 1939, months after war had been declared.

largest immediate impact that the war had on hundreds of Sheffield couples was not on those deciding what to see at the pictures, but on those waiting to get married who, because of the uncertainty of the times, were anxious to bring the date forward. It was reported that between 23 December and 26 December 1939 there were 113 weddings at Sheffield Registry Office which took place at the rate of eight an hour. A Superintendent of Registrars told a reporter that the majority of weddings were from the young members of the forces, who were marrying even though their very future was uncertain.

The Sheffield authorities recognised fairly early on that local industries were going to need more women than those who were single. Before the war it was expected that women who announced their intention to marry would leave any employment they had previously, but by July 1940 this attitude was turned on its head. Most active, married women were anxious to help in any way during the war and therefore when it was announced that there was work available for them, there was a grateful sigh all over the city. It was stated in the *Sheffield Telegraph* of 29 July that previously these women were hesitant to approach the employment authorities for fear that they would be enlisted, not into active service, but into the many knitting groups which had collected across the city. Now through sheer necessity, married women found themselves employed as secretaries, clerks, factory workers and shop assistants. Those who were interested in serving in a more military capacity flocked to sign up to join the Auxiliary Territorial Service (ATS) and other uniformed services. It was suggested that this was because many local women wanted to wear a uniform, in order to express their solidarity with those men already on active service. As a result there was a flood of applications towards units which wore uniforms, including those of ambulance drivers in the city. These women were trained by being taken on a practice run to judge their driving, they were to study the geographical area in which they would be based, and taught the basics of how to keep the ambulance clean, before being trained in first aid.

Other Sheffield women who could drive were recruited as taxi drivers in the beginning of September 1940. One of the first to be authorised was a young women called Millie Hawkesworth of Whitehouse Lane, Sheffield who was described as being tall and slim, 'wearing her auburn hair tossed back in an Eton crop'. She told a reporter that she had long been obsessed with cars and had wanted to be a mechanical engineer. At that time two other women were already in training to drive taxis, and after they were fully licensed they too would wear a uniform. The Sheffield employment authorities were also inviting applications for married or single women to become nurses or air-raid wardens. Others were encouraged to join the Women's Voluntary Service (WVS) which had many different roles from canteen work 'for the domesticated women' to the collection of clothes to be distributed to those who had lost everything in the bombing. Some of these women served tea to the survivors of Dunkirk when it was reported in the *Sheffield Telegraph* of 15 August 1940 that one of them told a reporter that she felt great sympathy for 'the men who were the same grim warriors that had stared death in the face just two months ago'. These brave Sheffield women of the WVS were put to the test between 1940–1942 when eighteen air raids took place over the city, damaging buildings and killing a great many people. For the duration of the war these women of the WVS tirelessly and courageously worked in rest shelters, serving meals and snacks to families who had lost everything. Despite having little sleep themselves, the women toiled to ensure that bombed out families had somewhere to sleep and something to eat after their ordeal. Thankfully their devotion to duty did not go unrewarded. After the particularly fearsome bombing on the nights of 12–15 December 1940, two women drivers from the Sheffield Air Raid Precautions (ARP) ambulance services were commended for their brave conduct. Mrs Susan Florence Harris of Union Road, Nether Edge and Miss Joan Brenda Sykes of Dykes Hall Road, Hillsborough received their medals for driving ambulances as the German bombs were falling cross the city.

What was not revealed until after the war was how significant Sheffield women had been in sharing Britain's radar triumph. Radar, called RDF (Radio and Direction Finding) had been around since the 1930s, and by the time the Battle of Britain was fought the RAF had fully integrated it into all of their aircraft. The radio factory of J.G. Graves Ltd at Crookes, Sheffield held 600 people who had been engaged on aircraft radio for the duration of the war. It was revealed that nine out of every ten workers were women aged from 14 to 60 years of age. The security secret was well-kept, until late August 1945 when it was revealed that both Sheffield housewives and young girls had been instrumental in supplying those radios. Ex-university technicians had been temporarily employed to train the women, and the scheme was so successful that both the Air Ministry and the RAF requested that they be employed full-time. The company were the main contractor for inter-unit cables for all radio and radar and as a result a large number of Bomber Command were fitted with the factory's products. Much of the simple elementary work was out-sourced to women working in shops and houses in the area, in groups of fifty or more. In this fashion many Sheffield women contributed to the success of the war. The workers of J.G. Graves Ltd were also engaged in the development of the cathode ray for the Air Ministry Research Department. These were later developed for use in television sets and computer monitors. Contracts from the RAF were issued, which modified and improved radar circuits used in the defence of Britain. As a recognition of the importance of the work, an award of a British Empire Medal was given to an employee Miss Annie Hall in the birthday honours.

Women who simply worked in shops were now able to step up to jobs previously only held by men. Mr Floyd of the Brightside and Carbrook Co-operative stores told one reporter that he now had twenty women working for him, and that he preferred women to his former employees. He found that they were more obliging than the male assistants, who had a more take-it-or-leave-it attitude to the customer. Instead he had found that female assistants took a real interest in the customer's requirements. He said, 'I find that our sales have doubled, even though we have fewer staff.' Other Sheffield women also took on more responsible positions. One woman who stepped into the breach during the war years was Miss Mary Winifred Middleham, who was appointed Assistant General Manager and Co-director with Mr Maurice Cole, of Messrs Cole Brothers of Sheffield. She had started work as an apprentice when she was 16 years of age, before becoming a buyer in the gowns department and then taking charge of the whole of the fashion section. Her rise was particularly welcomed by many of her customers, who spoke very positively about her helpful advice and pleasant friendly manner when serving customers.

One of the areas in which the women of Sheffield made history once again was in the local steelworks, in the production of munitions. The Minister of Supply, The Rt. Hon. Herbert Morrison MP had appealed to the people of the country and the factory managers in 'A Call for Arms' in May 1940. Once again, as in the Great War, more armaments were needed and Sheffield women flocked to produce tanks, weapons, steel helmets and shells. Factories such as Vickers, English Steel Co., Thomas Firth and John Brown's or Hadfield's steelworks worked long hours to provide these articles for the men at the front. Many of these heroic workers toiled for weeks on end without any holidays, in order to supply the tools needed to win the war. Although it was true that men were also employed in munitions, women had the responsibility of having to undertake a day's work before going home to clean and cook for their families. Their spirit created what is now celebrated as Sheffield's 'Women of Steel' who kept the foundry fires burning while all the time the air raids continued and bombs fell all around them. Even those women who were too old to go into the steelworks themselves, found roles in the works canteens serving food. As in the Great War the women working with their male colleagues had to get used to the obscene language on the factory floor, but they soon learned to give as good as they got, and relations between the two sexes became a little less strained. Once again the naive teenagers, married and single women found themselves working on pay that was half as much as men would receive, but there were few complaints. They trained to undertake jobs operating heavy machinery using hammers, and furnaces and driving heavy vehicles previously thought only suitable for men. *Sheffield Independent* columnist Margaret Simpson spoke about the courage of these women when they held an ARP practice in one of the largest munitions works in August 1940. Simpson spoke to the women and found that it was a matter of pride to them and other workers that they arrived to start their shifts on time, no matter how badly bombed the city had been the night before. Because of the damage to the transport systems, many of them had an hour's trek through rubble left from damaged houses, to get to their machines before their working day began. Often as the women set off from their homes, they had no idea if their factory was still standing among the ruins of the city. Simpson went to visit some of these female steelworkers again in March 1941 who proudly told her that work does not always stop when the sirens go off. She described how there was

> a glow in the eye of these begrimed girls, who look queerly coltish and young in their boiler suits, doing with consummate skill work on machinery hitherto only done by men. With a superb gay indifference to enemy activity, these girls continue to work if the sirens go. They laugh at danger.

The columnist described the whirl and clatter of machinery which interminably continued, yielding more and more of the required war materiel and how the girls' nimble fingers were accurate to a thousandth part of an inch. She told her readers that many have husbands who are in the forces, widows of men killed in the war or whose husbands were holding down civilian war jobs, but they all had to toughen up when working together. Many experienced for the first time a new culture of people working together, developing such a rapport with each other that was not dimmed by working alongside industrial-sized rats. Through it all the women found a sense of camaraderie and unity that many had not experienced previously, and many felt liberated for the first time.

One girl named Edith Plummer of Greenhill Road, Sheffield told a reporter from the *Sheffield Daily Telegraph* that she was a London girl and had never been in a factory before the war. Nevertheless she now found that she loved the work and the people of the city and she fully intended to make her permanent home in Sheffield. Another 'Woman of Steel' was 20-year-old Gladys Brand (nee Wakefield), whose mother had died around 1935 leaving her and her younger sister to be brought up by their father. She too had applied to the Labour Exchange for work, and like many other young, single woman before her had no say in where she wanted to be employed. As a result Gladys was sent to train at Rotherham Technical College, Howard Street, Rotherham, to learn about micrometers, lathes and basic fitting skills before starting work at a firm called Darwin's at

Gladys Wakefield as a young woman.

Gladys Brand today.

Templeborough. She had not been employed before the war, so this was her first job, as she donned a smock and wound a turban around her hair. Gladys worked mornings, afternoon and night shifts making shells, and when the air-raid siren went off, some of the women would gather up their tin hats and go down into the cellar, which had been converted into an air-raid shelter for the workers.

Yet many of the workers felt that their work was too important and many worked through the air raids, staying by their machines. Some of these workers were entertained by Gracie Fields in August 1941 when she came to a munitions factory in Sheffield. Workers climbed up ladders and perched on girders 20-feet-high above the ground to ensure a good vantage point to see the star of radio and film. In the centre of this enthusiastic mass of men and women stood Gracie, dressed in a white blouse and tartan skirt. But when she started to sing she stunned them all by not singing the songs she became most famous for, but instead gave a rendition of the 'Lords Prayer'. The whole canteen joined in as men took off their caps in respect. After just another two songs the audience were clamouring for her to sing 'Sally' and she agreed telling them 'Come on lads and lasses. Lets forget we're in t' factory', as she sang not only 'Sally' but her other hit of the time 'Walter' conducting the audience herself. Gracie Fields was reported as doing three visits a day to various works all over the country, but said that she would never forget the warm welcome she received at Sheffield. Yet when the war ended these women who had kept the steel and munitions works running ceaselessly, were fired without a word of thanks. Some were given a few days notice, whilst others were kept on long enough to show the man who was replacing them, how to run the machines. It had always been made very clear that they would only be necessary until the servicemen came home at the end of the war, but to many it was a severe blow. Gone overnight was the camaraderie and the long friendships carved from working closely together. During this war, more so than the First World War, women had proved pivotal to making history. They had been used to develop Radar, had shown their mettle at handling heavy barrage balloons, when detractors stated that they were not physically equipped to do the job.

Throughout the years from 1850 to 1950 the women of Sheffield had been on a long journey. As the 1950s dawned there were some improvements in their lives. More sympathy was shown by the legal authorities towards women suffering from domestic violence, although the reasons for one partner's violence towards another would take much longer to understand. Women now sat as magistrates, become part of a jury and were employed as doctors, solicitors or probation officers. As mothers they now had access to health services for themselves and their children as well as ways of limiting their families, but in Sheffield many things took much longer to change. Even in the 1950s a woman's primary duty was to stay at home, look after the children and make a comfortable home for her husband. If she was working it was understood that she would leave her job when she got married. Although divorces were easier to obtain, it was not until 1957 that proof of a marriage irretrievably breaking down could be accepted as a reason. The man was still the accepted head of the house and usually had control over the cheque book and bank accounts. At that time a married woman could not sign a hire purchase agreement or get a mortgage without her husband's consent.

In schools the gender lines were rigidly enforced with boys learning traditional craft work, whilst women were taught more domestic tasks. Sheffield even had 'men only' pubs where women were banned, and the Sunday dinner time session was sacrosanct for men, whilst their wives stayed at home and cooked the dinner. Another Yorkshire tradition which was prevalent in Sheffield was that few wives knew what their husbands earned and only he decided how much 'housekeeping' he would allow her every week, keeping the remainder for himself. Once again women had to turn this around. Many of these strong Sheffield matriarchs ensured better equality for their daughters by encouraging them to become educated, and therefore gaining more employment prospects than they themselves had. Thanks to the suffragettes, women were now able to enter the political arena ensuring better lives for the next generation of the city's females.

Perhaps the biggest tribute to Sheffield women came from beyond the scope of this book, but it is so important a milestone to their achievements that it is difficult to leave out. At the end of 2010 a movement was brought by the *Star* newspaper to have some form of recognition for the thousands of Sheffield women working in the steelworks as munitions workers during both world wars. As we have seen, throughout the years of the war they had kept Sheffield steelworks producing essential materials through the country's darkest hours. At the end of both wars these local women had been given no recognition and had simply been handed their cards and sent home to resume their former lives, and the *Star* felt that they needed some form of thanks. The scheme was initiated by Kathleen Turner, one of the workers who had worked in the steelworks in the Second World War. She had contacted the newspaper, stating that she was fiercely proud of the role she and other Sheffield women had taken. As she said: 'The Land Army were praised for feeding us, but we did the same by keeping the boys supplied with what they needed. If we hadn't done that they wouldn't have got the tanks and fighter planes needed.'

No one was quite sure how many women of Sheffield had been employed during the Second World War, let alone how many were still alive, accepting that most of them would be in their eighties and nineties at that time. Women who read about the campaign resulted in the *Star* receiving many calls within hours of the paper being for sale on the streets. As a result, a delegation of four women went to 10 Downing Street to speak with Prime Minister, Gordon Brown on 13 January 2010. Because of their actions, the women of Sheffield were now headline news on *BBC News at Ten*, and some had their faces and their accounts published in national newspapers. Due to the secrecy following the war when most ordinary people just wanted to forget, many of the accounts had never been heard of before. Subsequently local families were stunned to learn that a relative had even been inside a steelworks, let alone spent much of the war working twelve-hour shifts there. But through all the accounts came the development of incredible bonds formed between the Sheffield women as together they faced incredible dangers as they worked.

As a result, on 17 June 2016 a bronze statue was unveiled in Sheffield at Barkers Pool, dedicated to the 'Women of Steel'. The statue had been sculpted by Martin Jennings, and over 100 of the, now elderly, women were in the crowd. Councillor Julie Dore spoke for the city when she told the assembled crowd:

> There was a war on, they were taking care of their families, and missing their husbands and fathers. But they went to work every day in the steelworks to do difficult physical labour in hot, noisy conditions that we couldn't imagine today. They deserve our respect and our thanks. I am delighted to speak on behalf of the whole city and say thank you to Sheffield's incredible women of steel.

☆**The Star** front page, January 14th, 2010

■ They worked through the Second World War
■ When peace-time came they lost their jobs
■ They never got any thanks for their efforts
■ But finally – after 65 years – the PM says ...

PM's tribute: Gordon Brown with, from the left, Dorothy Slingsby, Kitty Sollitt, Kathleen Roberts and Ruby Gascoigne at No 10   Picture: Sarah Washbourn

THANK YOU

NANCY FIELDER
News Reporter

"WELL done!"

Prime Minister Gordon Brown welcomed our Women of Steel into Downing Street to thank them personally for their service to the country.

And Mr Brown heaped praised on The Star for our massively successful campaign.

The women who kept South Yorkshire's steelworks and factories going during World War II finally received official recognition yesterday for their dedication as well as personal thanks from the very top.

Our delegation took London by storm and hit the national headlines during an extraordinary day organised by Sheffield MP Richard Caborn.

Kathleen Roberts, Kit Sollitt, Dorothy Slingsby and Ruby

Gascoigne were given VIP treatment at the Ministry of Defence, Parliament and No 10.

The Prime Minister said: "I am delighted to welcome Sheffield's

'Women of Steel' to No 10 and to have the chance to thank some of these incredible women in person for their sterling service during WWII.

"We are extremely grateful for the huge contribution they made to the war effort. Their striking stories show the crucial role they played in difficult and sometimes dangerous conditions.

"South Yorkshire and the whole

▶ **Continues on Page 3**

Front page of the Star *on 14 January 2010.*

Women of Steel *statue in Barkers Pool.*

There is little more to say. The women of Sheffield have shown their mettle, not only fighting injustices of inequality and gaining political status, but also in bringing those injustices to the attention of the public. Their actions, whether fighting on the streets of the city or standing behind machines making armaments which would win the war have, without doubt, made the city proud.

Bibliography

Books

Murphy, Molly, *Molly Murphy: Suffragette and Socialist* (1998)

Price, David, *Sheffield Troublemakers: Rebels and Radicals in Sheffield History* (Phillimore, 2008)

The Star Salutes Our Women of Steel: The Girls who kept the Foundry Fires Burning (2010)

Newspaper Sources

Northern Star & Leeds General Advertiser

Reynolds's Newspaper

Sheffield Independent

Sheffield Daily Telegraph

Sheffield Evening Telegraph

Sheffield Telegraph

Sheffield and Rotherham Independent

Star

Online Resources

The Vote – Suffragette Magazine operating from 1910 to November 1933

https://news.google.com/newspapers?nid=O3NaXM p0MMsC&dat=19110107& printsec=frontpage&hl=en

Sheffield Archives Sources

House of Help Case Books (Ref: 158/5/1/1 & 2)

100 Years Forward: A Century of the House of Help, Sheffield: The Oldest Hostel for Women (Ref: X158/6/7a/7b)

Magistrates Court Register, July 1882–August 1884 (Ref: MC1/1)

Magistrates Court Register, May 1913–December 1915 (Ref: MC/3/8)

ASLEF Minute Book 1915–1919, 12 November 1916 (Ref: ASLEF/1b)

Sheffield Local Studies Sources

Sheffield Year Book and Record for 1884–1896 (Ref: 032.74S)

Sheffield Year Book and Record for 1910–1928 (Ref: 032.74S)

Copies of *The Bombshell* magazine dated Christmas 1917, January 1918 and November 1918 Victory Edition, October 1919 (Ref 052.74S)

Courtesy of Alice Collins

Sheffield Women's History Walk: Sheffield Women's History Group

Index